D1083054

ON INHUMANITY

Praise for *On Inhumanity*

"*On Inhumanity* is a powerful exploration of the processes and consequences of dehumanization. Concerning himself with violence and the processes that motivate the extermination of 'lesser beings,' Smith pens a much-needed treatment of the constantly reemerging brutality that is seemingly endemic to the human condition. . . Simply put, *On Inhumanity* is a most appropriate confrontation with the illusions and political powers that produce sub-humanity in the 21st century."— Tommy J. Curry, University of Edinburgh, author of *The Man-Not*

"*On Inhumanity* profoundly interrogates the processes that lead [or what leads] ordinary people to engage in horrific acts of violence against others. Tracing common themes across the Holocaust, lynching, and genocides, Smith identifies dehumanization—seeing human beings as subhuman creatures—as the central feature of these mass atrocities, as well as of everyday forms of racial oppression. Most compelling is that Smith refuses to conclude that dehumanization is our inevitable destiny and instead charts a course for resisting it. *On Inhumanity* brilliantly provides a chilling warning of repeating the past and a hopeful call to create a more humane future."—Dorothy Roberts, University of Pennsylvania Carey Law School, author of *Fatal Invention*

"A chilling, comprehensive, and passionate account of dehumanisation. Smith offers a devastating reminder of the capacity of every human to treat other humans as lesser."—Angela Saini, journalist, author of *Inferior* and *Superior*

ON INHUMANITY

Dehumanization and How to Resist It

David Livingstone Smith

OXFORD
UNIVERSITY PRESS

Oxford University Press is a department of the University of Oxford. It furthers
the University's objective of excellence in research, scholarship, and education
by publishing worldwide. Oxford is a registered trade mark of Oxford University
Press in the UK and certain other countries.

Published in the United States of America by Oxford University Press
198 Madison Avenue, New York, NY 10016, United States of America.

© Oxford University Press 2020

Epigraph from THE SOCIAL CONQUEST OF EARTH
by Edward O. Wilson. Copyright © 2012 Edward O. Wilson.
Used by permission of Liveright Publishing Corporation.

Library of Congress Cataloging-in-Publication Data
Names: Smith, David Livingstone, 1953– author.
Title: On inhumanity : dehumanization and how to resist it /
David Livingstone Smith.
Description: New York, NY : Oxford University Press, 2020. |
Includes index.
Identifiers: LCCN 2019048933 (print) | LCCN 2019048934 (ebook) |
ISBN 9780190923006 (hb) | ISBN 9780190923020 (epub) | ISBN 9780190092566 (online)
Subjects: LCSH: Humanity—Psychological aspects. | Cruelty. | Hate. | Toleration.
Classification: LCC HM1131 .S653 2020 (print) | LCC HM1131 (ebook) |
DDC 179/.9—dc23
LC record available at https://lccn.loc.gov/2019048933
LC ebook record available at https://lccn.loc.gov/2019048934

9 8 7 6 5 4 3 2 1

Printed by Sheridan Books, Inc., United States of America

For Subrena, twenty-two years on.

Humanity is a magnificent but fragile achievement.

EDWARD O. WILSON

CONTENTS

ACKNOWLEDGMENTS

I want to thank Adam Hochman for his expertise, Sasha Smith and Abigail Erickson for the words to say things, Desireé Melton and John Kaag for their unflagging encouragement, Darien Pollock for his street disposition, Rosa Pollock for her seal of approval, Mat Schlissler and Kayleigh Long for sharing their knowledge of Myanmar, Robin Dembroff for their expertise on gender, Lucy Randall for making the whole thing happen (and for her superb editing), and Subrena Smith for much more than I can ever put into words.

ACKNOWLEDGMENTS

ON INHUMANITY

| INTRODUCTION

The Deep South at the tail end of the Jim Crow era was organized around the idea that Whites deserved power, privilege, and any resources they demanded, while anyone else, especially Blacks, were born to a life sentence of inferiority. This was the world in which I grew up. Raw racial oppression was all around. In public buildings and supermarkets, signs indicated White vs. Black water fountains—those reserved for Whites clean and well-maintained, and those for Blacks dirty, rusty, and in disrepair. The local beach—a beautiful one, on the Gulf of Mexico—was for Whites only, as was clear from the sign telling visitors that neither Negroes nor dogs were allowed. Our town was segregated, with Black people living in dire poverty in an area known as Dunbar Heights, far from the protected domain of White families. And I recall seeing crews of Black prisoners laboring by the roadside in the blistering Florida sun, under the eyes of armed White prison guards.

These common signs of a world built to privilege Whites and oppress Blacks did not just reflect what the government wanted or what the rules required. Most of the people who inhabited my

world—the White section of a sleepy southern town—were mari-
nated from birth to death in the ideology that racial oppression is
part of the natural order of things. And they enacted this ideology
in their daily lives. The White children whom I played with, as
well as their parents and grandparents, regarded Black people as
subhuman. Sometimes this was explicit, as when boys I went to
high school with boasted of hunting Black kids with their pellet
guns on weekends. Mostly it was unspoken, but nevertheless as
palpable and suffocating as the humid, heavy air.

My family's place in this racially riven world was more complicated than it may have seemed on the surface. My mother was
the daughter of Jewish immigrants—or, I should say, refugees—
from Eastern Europe, whose families looked to America as a safe
haven from the pogroms. Her parents, Chaim, who was born in
Belarus, and Bertha, who was born in Romania, were brilliant,
self-educated people who had to quit school early: he to work in
a Coca-Cola bottling plant, and she—at the age of fourteen—to
work in a sweatshop on the Lower East Side of New York City
(at the time, nicknamed "The Ghetto"). They visited us each
summer.

Eventually, after my parents divorced, my grandparents left
Brooklyn and moved down South to live with us. I grew up in their
loving presence, and they taught me about the horrors of history.
Some were family stories. There was the story of Chaim's mother
giving birth to him while hidden in a haystack while the Jews in
her village were being raped and slaughtered. She was gagged, so
she could not cry out in pain. And there was the story of Bertha's
mother, Rose, who fled anti-Semitic persecution to live deep in the
Romanian forest with a group of Roma that took her in. I heard

that she was once pushed off the sidewalk into the muddy gutter by a gentile soldier who snarled, "Get off the sidewalk, Jew!" (According to family legend, she looked him dead in the eye and cursed him: "You will die before the sun sets!"—which, of course, in the reassuring family fable, he did.)

Others were historical. My grandmother read incessantly, and shared her encyclopedic knowledge with me. She taught me about the history of brutal oppression of Black Americans, which helped me make sense of the world in which I found myself, and although she couldn't bear to talk about the Holocaust (when someone mentioned the word "German" she would curse in Yiddish and spit), she taught me about the history of anti-Semitism. Most of all, she had a vast knowledge of Native American history, and taught me about the history of the American genocide without whitewashing it.

My father was a different character entirely. He was born in Brazil, of missionary parents from an old southern family. He was a kind, quiet man, whose spirit was crushed by his rigid Christian upbringing. He struggled with his own racial prejudices all his life, which isn't surprising, given his background. When my father fell in love with a Black girl in his early teens, his alarmed parents sent him away to the ancestral home in Belton, South Carolina, to sever their budding relationship. He never saw her again. It was in South Carolina that he first met his grandfather Wilbur, a Confederate veteran of the American Civil War (a map that Wilbur drew in 1862, while on a campaign in Virginia, hangs on my study wall). Wilbur's father, Aaron, had been a perpetrator in Andrew Jackson's genocidal expulsion of the Cherokees from Georgia. Racism ran in the family, but, at least to a certain extent, it began to end with my father, who married a Jewish woman, my mother, at the end of World War II.

After getting married in Brooklyn, the newlyweds drove down to Belton for their honeymoon. The locals, who did not have a high opinion of Jews, freely referred to my mother as the Whore of Babylon. (I once found an old family picture from which the image of my mother was literally excised with a pair of scissors.) My dad—who worked as a manual laborer, but was also a lay preacher—was invited to deliver a sermon in the local Methodist church. He decided to preach against the Ku Klux Klan. Later that day, there was a loud knock on the door. It was the local sheriff, judge, and preacher—all of whom, it turned out, were Klan members. They told him if he knew what was good for him he'd get out of town. He did.

All these experiences, memories, and stories—and many others, too numerous to mention here—shaped my outlook on the world. While working to untangle the complexity of dehumanization and its many horrendous consequences throughout history through today, I keep in mind that although my family tree included strong and resilient people who fled oppression, it also links me just as strongly to those who fought and killed to protect a brutally oppressive world. Many years after sitting with my grandparents and hearing their nightmarish stories, as a grown man and an academic, their influence led me to study the darker and more troubling sides of being human—deception, violence, racism, and dehumanization. This culminated in my 2011 book, *Less Than Human: Why We Demean, Enslave, and Exterminate Others*, which both pulled together the history of dehumanization from ancient times to the present and developed a theory of how dehumanization works. In it, I explored what it is about the human mind that makes it possible for us to see other people as less than human, and to treat them cruelly as a result.

Less Than Human was my first attempt at setting out a comprehensive history and theory of dehumanization. Since writing it, my views about how dehumanization works have evolved and become more sophisticated, and that's why I decided to write this book. I've written *On Inhumanity* for a very broad audience, because the topic of dehumanization is too important to be hidden away in the pages of academic journals and esoteric books that hardly anyone reads—especially now. With each passing year the task of understanding it, and conveying this understanding to others, becomes more pressing. There has been an upswing in authoritarian politics all over the world, which continues to gather momentum. White nationalist groups are surging in both the United States and Europe, and hate crimes against vulnerable minorities are on the increase. Combine this with the impending threat of catastrophic climate change, which, even at conservative estimates of its effects, will result in a refugee crisis that is unequaled in human history, and we are looking at a perfect storm for dehumanization and mass atrocity.

Dehumanization is extremely dangerous. It's something that we should all do our utmost to resist. But to resist dehumanization, you've got to be able to recognize it and understand its inner workings. In the pages to follow, I've done my best to raise awareness of these issues in a clear and accessible, yet rigorous, way. I've avoided technical jargon and in-text citation as much as possible, but I've included a section at the end of the book recommending additional sources for those readers who want to pursue more deeply the topics that I address.

If we want to eliminate dehumanization, it's crucial to figure out what it is about human beings—all human beings—that enables us to conceive of others as less than human. But there's also a tendency that goes in the opposite direction. Instead of putting the process of dehumanization under a magnifying glass, *there's a tendency to castigate those who dehumanize others as evil monsters*—to dehumanize the dehumanizers—and thus to indulge in the very form of thinking that one ostensibly seeks to combat. Describing other human beings as monsters is an obstacle to seriously addressing the problem. It doesn't matter how repugnant or destructive their beliefs and actions are. Monsters are fictional, but dehumanizers are real, and they are mostly ordinary people like you and me. (I saw this as a child, and rediscovered it in my research decades later.) Indeed, it's something of a cliché to say that, given the right circumstances, virtually all of us are capable of slipping into the dehumanizing mindset, and committing acts of cruelty that would otherwise be difficult or even impossible for us to perform. This admission, however heartfelt, doesn't take us very far unless we're prepared to seriously engage with the question of exactly what it is about us that makes dehumanization not only possible, but often highly tempting.

These points have important implications for how to resist dehumanization. Resisting dehumanization takes place on two fronts. One part is resisting the dehumanizing impulse *in ourselves*. To do that, you've got to acknowledge that you're capable of dehumanizing others, and you've got to have knowledge of what it is about the human mind—what it is about *your* mind—that disposes us to regard our fellow human beings as less than human. But the psychological dimension is only half the story. The other half is social and political.

In this book, I try to do justice to both aspects of resisting dehumanization, because they're so entangled with one another. It's impossible to make sense of dehumanization purely as a political phenomenon, because dehumanization involves human behavior, and for political forces to affect human behavior they have to interface with our psychology. Likewise, dehumanization can't be explained psychologically in isolation from the political surround. Thinking of others as less than human isn't something that arises spontaneously from within as a response to "difference." Those who try to explain dehumanization, racism, and other related phenomena psychologically as natural antagonisms toward "outgroups" lose sight of the fact that ingroups and outgroups are political creations rather than brute facts of nature. You can't make sense of the notions of "us" and "them"—much less "human" and "subhuman"—if you don't include propaganda and ideology as part of the equation.

I'd like to imagine that this book will make some difference, however miniscule, to the conduct of human affairs. Perhaps this hope is foolishly optimistic. I would like to think that many people will read it and take its message to heart. But I'm also painfully aware that for a general-audience book to succeed, it helps to deliver an upbeat message—for instance, that we can eliminate dehumanization by taking several easy steps, that the future looks rosy, and so on. The problem is, I can't in good conscience do that. This is intended as a *constructive* book—a book that tries to tackle an enormously difficult and serious problem—rather than a book that ignores the difficulty and seriousness of the problem in favor of cheap reassurances. I confess that I'm not optimistic about our collective future. I think that, given the looming threat of catastrophic climate change, and the devastating social consequences that are sure to follow in its wake, a descent into the worst sort of barbarism is overwhelmingly likely before the century is out.

There is a brutally poignant Jewish joke—one that stabs you in the heart rather than makes you laugh—about Sol, the village idiot. Because of Sol's intellectual deficits, he is regarded as unemployable. But the village Rabbi, undeterred, creates a job for him. Sol's job is to sit on a chair on the outskirts of the *shtetl* and wait for the Messiah to arrive. One day a traveler approaches, and seeing Sol sitting there, all alone, staring intently into the distance, the traveler asks him what he's doing. "It's my job," says Sol. "I'm waiting for the Messiah. The pay is bad and the hours are long, but it's steady work."

Perhaps I am a fool like Sol, because despite my pessimism I am nonetheless hopeful that we may be able to see our way through to making a more humane world, and fashion a future that is less hideous than the nightmare of our past.

2 | WHY DEHUMANIZATION MATTERS

The Rwanda genocide of 1994 was one of the worst bloodbaths of the twentieth century. Over the course of three months, militant members of the Hutu ethnic majority rose up, and, machetes in hand, did their best to exterminate the Tutsi minority, hunting down and killing nearly a million of them. During the lead-up to the genocide, and also while it was unfolding, Hutu propaganda characterized the Tutsi as cockroaches and snakes. Was this mere derogatory name calling? The testimony of some killers suggests otherwise. "We no longer saw a human being when we turned up a Tutsi in the swamps," said one. "They did not even see that it was a human being that they were busy killing," said another. And yet another said, "We no longer considered the Tutsis as humans or even as creatures of God."[1] Although these men told their interlocutor that the genocidaires didn't *see* human victims beneath the blades of their machetes, they didn't mean to imply that they were suffering from hallucinations or had defective vision. They meant to say that they didn't see these people *as* human beings. When the killers looked at their victims, they didn't see anything that you and I wouldn't see. They saw beings with a human form, beings who in every observable respect were indistinguishable from those whom we regard as human beings. But the killers *interpreted* what they saw differently than how you and I would. They believed that the humanity of these others was only skin deep. They thought that these people merely appeared human—much like counterfeit money appears to be real money—*but that their victims were not really human. They were something else. Something that's malevolent and despicable. Something that needs killing.*

Genocide is the most disturbing example of dehumanization's destructive power. It follows a regular pattern, time and time again. First the dominant majority singles out an ethnic or racial minority as a threat. They label them murderers, rapists, or freeloading parasites sucking the life out of the body of the state. Next, they subject them to discrimination and abuse, segregate them, and humiliate them. Finally—and this step is crucial to the emergence of full-blown genocidal violence—they no longer see and treat the victims as human beings, but as filthy, subhuman creatures that must be eradicated, ravenous predators that must be hunted down, or animals to be tamed, abused, and exploited.

Why should anyone care about dehumanization? Dehumanization fuels the worst brutalities that human beings perpetrate against one another. It's not just a problem of the modern, industrialized world: it's haunted humanity for millennia. We find traces of it in writings from the ancient civilizations of Egypt, China, and Mesopotamia, in Medieval European characterizations of Jews, and Medieval Arabs' characterizations of Black Africans, and in far-flung indigenous cultures, such as the headhunting

Munduruku people of Brazil who referred to their human prey as *pariwat*—a word that's otherwise reserved for game animals.

Dehumanization is a worldwide problem with deep historical roots, but it is also a *growing* problem around the world that promises to worsen in a future in which climate crises will turn more and more of us into refugees on foreign soil. In order to know how to deal with the problem of dehumanization, we have to understand what it is and how it works.

Dehumanization isn't only a factor in genocide. It also creeps into how we think of enemies during wartime, and wartime propaganda often zeros in on the dehumanizing mindset, exploiting the chinks in our psychological armor. For most people, killing others isn't something that's easy to do. For most of us, there are massive psychological barriers that must be overcome before we can find it in ourselves to pull a lethal trigger or plunge a blade into a person's viscera. To surmount these barriers, wartime propaganda presents "our" cause as a morally righteous one that no decent human being should have qualms about participating in. The story's been told many times and in many places: we kill to save the world, to stamp out evil, to liberate, to keep us free. But even those who've drunk the patriotic Kool-Aid are likely to find it hard to take the lives of others. So, propagandists, such as the militant Hutus, as we saw, often deploy another, different rhetorical strategy. They represent the enemy as subhuman.

World War II is an especially rich source for examples of dehumanizing propaganda, and not just by our enemies. "We are not dealing with humans as we know them . . . ," remarked Sir Thomas A. Blamey, commander of the Allied land forces in New Guinea, in an interview on the front page of the *New York Times*.

"We are dealing with something primitive. Our troops have the right view of the Japs. They regard them as vermin."[2] Another chilling example appeared in 1944 in *Leatherneck* magazine, a US Marine Corps publication, in an ostensibly lighthearted article entitled "Bugs That Every Marine Should Know." The article included a drawing of a parasite with an insect-like body and a grotesquely caricatured Japanese face. A caption states that this nasty little creature is *Louseus japanicus*: the Japanese louse. The accompanying text says that a "lice epidemic" began with the attack on Pearl Harbor, and that the Marine Corps, who are specially trained to combat this "pestilence," are assigned the task of "extermination." It goes on to say, "Flame throwers, mortars, grenades and bayonets have proven to be an effective remedy. But before a complete cure may be effected, the origin of the plague, the breeding grounds around the Tokyo area, must be completely destroyed."[3]

The article appeared during the very month that US military forces firebombed Tokyo. Over sixteen hundred tons of incendiary bombs turned sixteen square miles of the most densely populated area of the city into an inferno. One hundred thousand or more men, women, and children literally vanished into ashes. And this was just the beginning of a massive bombing campaign, unparalleled in its ferocity, which culminated in the obliteration of Hiroshima and Nagasaki with nuclear weapons. Through the seemingly innocuous, lighthearted cartoon, soldiers were being urged to consider the enemy as *other*, not as people whose children and families and homes would be destroyed by US military action, but as a different, lesser, repulsive class of creature—one that deserved to be wiped off the earth.

Dehumanization played a large role in the Pacific theater because race was a factor. Predominantly White allied soldiers dehumanized the Japanese as rats, apes, monkeys, and insects—but had no such attitudes toward the Germans, whom they considered as men of their own race. The difference in attitudes produced a difference in behavior. American soldiers sometimes mutilated the bodies of the Japanese dead, cutting out bones, and even whole skulls, de-fleshing them, and keeping them as souvenirs, or sending them to friends and family back home, but I don't know of a single episode of American troops taking German body parts as hunting trophies. People tend not to mutilate those whom they regard as their own kind.

The war in Vietnam was another arena where dehumanization was rampant. Soldiers thought of the Vietnamese as subhuman animals. Nick Turse explains in *Kill Everything That Moves: The Real American War in Vietnam* that this was known to military personnel as the "mere-gook rule," which held that "all Vietnamese . . . were little more than animals, who could be killed or abused at will."

> Some soldiers hacked off the heads of Vietnamese to keep, trade, or exchange for prizes offered by commanders. Many more cut off the ears of their victims. . . . Some of these trophies were presented to superiors as gifts or as proofs to confirm a body count. Others were retained . . . and worn on necklaces or otherwise displayed. While ears were the most common souvenirs of this type, scalps, penises, noses, breasts, teeth, and fingers were also favored.[4]

As Vietnam War veteran Stan Groff notes, dehumanization of the enemy helps in the gruesome business of killing. Discussing his combat experiences, he says, "we had to dehumanize our victims before we did the things we did. . . ." He continues:

> So, they became dinks or gooks, just like Iraqis are now being transformed into ragheads or hajjis. People had to be reduced to "niggers" here before they could be lynched. No difference. We convinced ourselves we had to kill them to survive, even when that wasn't true, but something inside us told us that so long as they were human beings, with the same intrinsic value we had as human beings, we were not allowed to burn their homes and barns, kill their animals, and sometimes even kill them. So we used these words, these new names, to reduce them, to strip them of their essential humanity, and then we could do things like adjust artillery fire onto the cries of a baby.[5]

Dehumanization isn't always in the service of slaughter. It's also the handmaid of oppression. We find its bloodstained fingerprints all over chattel slavery.

It was common for North American slaveholders to think of the human beings whom they enslaved as belonging to a lower species of animal—a notion of racial hierarchy that was part of a more encompassing, hierarchical vision of the cosmos, which I discuss in chapter eleven. Because Black people were seen as subhuman, this made it acceptable for White slavers to treat them as their livestock. And after the end of Civil War, Whites depicted Black people—in particular Black men—as primitive, voracious beasts, bent on rape and murder. This fueled the mass atrocity of lynching, when Black men were tortured, grotesquely mutilated, and burned to death before cheering crowds (sometimes numbering in the thousands) of White men, women, and even children. Some of the victims had the skin stripped from their body, or had their fingers and toes cut off and taken away by Whites as souvenirs. Some were forced to eat their own severed genitals. In one case, a tortured women's unborn baby was cut out of her belly and stomped to death.

There were more than four thousand recorded lynchings of Black people in the United States between 1877 and 1950, and there were many more—nobody knows how many more—that went unrecorded. Hundreds of African Americans were also lynched in the North and West. And other racialized groups were also targeted and lynched in the hundreds or thousands: Mexicans, Native Americans, and Chinese, as well as Whites who violated the strict rules of the racial hierarchy.

The attitudes that fueled lynching aren't just relics from an ignorant and intolerant past. A full century after the first recorded spectacle lynching (the lynching of Henry Smith in 1893), influential White Americans, including prominent academics and the then First Lady Hillary Clinton, were still characterizing young black men as *superpredators*—savage beasts in human form. And later still, in the second decade of the twenty-first century, the then presidential candidate and later president, Donald Trump, described undocumented immigrants who cross our southern border as rapists, murderers, and *animals*, to the fervent ovation of his supporters (I will say more about this in chapter twenty-three).

Once we begin to learn about dehumanization—its mechanics, its history, its uncanny destructive power—we see it everywhere and further appreciate the urgency of opposing it. In the chapters to follow, I'll be moving backward and forward in time, visiting historical examples of dehumanization to mine from them lessons about how dehumanization works in the present. I will also be using present-day psychological research to make sense of the actions of those who, in decades and centuries past, thought of other human beings as less than human.

It's all too easy to minimize the significance of dehumanization by thinking of it as a relic of the past or as something that only other people do. But dehumanizing attitudes, and the violence that they breed, have shaped modern societies, including our own, and they live on in the present. Recognizing this, and taking dehumanization seriously, is the first step toward combatting it.

3 | DEFINING DEHUMANIZATION

Google the word "dehumanization" and you will get more than 8 million hits. Read further, and you'll find that many of these explicitly or implicitly define the term, and you'll also discover that many of those definitions conflict. Some say that dehumanizing others is the same as treating them in a cruel, degrading, or humiliating way. Others say that dehumanization is a kind of derogatory speech—the use of slurs to denigrate or demonize whole groups of people. Still others hold that dehumanization means thinking of others as inferior or not fully human, or as inanimate objects. And this short list doesn't exhaust the options.

Of course, there's some connection between all these meanings, but it's a very loose one. They all pertain to something that's wrong or degrading, but that's pretty much where the similarity ends. Each of these notions of dehumanization is logically independent of the others, which means that they don't overlap.

Take the first notion of dehumanization that I mentioned: the idea that to dehumanize someone is to deliberately treat them in cruel, humiliating, or degrading ways. Now, compare this to the last one on my list: the idea that when we dehumanize others we conceive of them as lifeless objects. It's easy to see that these are completely different ideas. The first one describes a way of *treating* people, whereas the second describes a way of *thinking* about them. And notice that the idea of being cruel to an inanimate object doesn't make any sense. To treat another cruelly—for instance, by torturing them—is to deliberately cause them to suffer. But inanimate objects don't have feelings and can't suffer. You can't torture a washing machine. Similarly, you can only humiliate a being if they are capable of self-respect. But inanimate objects aren't capable of self-respect. You can't humiliate a flower pot. So, thinking of others as inanimate objects *rules out* deliberately treating them in cruel or degrading ways.

This is just one example of the large gaps that exist between different conceptions of dehumanization, which can make discussions very confusing. If I mean one thing by "dehumanization" and you mean something else by the word, then we're unlikely to have a fruitful conversation. Because grappling with dehumanization is so very important, this situation shouldn't be tolerated.

Confusion about the meaning of dehumanization is a lot more consequential than many other philosophical confusions are. Debates about many traditional philosophical topics—for instance, the nature of truth, or beauty, or the question of whether there is an objective world outside of our own minds—are of little importance for the living of human lives. Trying to achieve clarity about such subjects is a wonderful intellectual exercise, but it's definitely a low-stakes game. In contrast, the consequences of confusion about dehumanization are potentially far more drastic and devastating. We're not just playing word games here or solving intellectual puzzles when we're trying to make sense of dehumanization. Treating it seriously is more an obligation than an option.

Anyone who aims to address the phenomenon of dehumanization seriously needs to do two things right from the start. First, they should be explicit about what they mean by "dehumanization." They shouldn't be vague or hand-wavy or rely on the assumption that everyone understands what's being talked about. They should lay it on the line as clearly and precisely as possible. And second, they should make the case why this notion of dehumanization is preferable to the other options that are on the table.

I see dehumanization as a kind of attitude—a way of thinking about others. *To dehumanize another person is to conceive of them as a subhuman creature.* There's a lot more content condensed in this short sentence than might be apparent, and I'll be unpacking it in the chapters to follow. But for now, I'd just like you to keep your eye on the definitional ball. When I talk about dehumanization I mean this and nothing else.

People often mistake dehumanization for its effects on human behavior. This muddies the water and makes it much more difficult to comprehend how dehumanization works. When people think of others as subhuman, they often treat them in cruel and degrading ways, and they often refer to them using slurs. But bad treatment and degrading slurs are effects of dehumanization rather than dehumanization itself. They are, so to speak, symptoms of the disease, rather than the disease itself. And you can't cure a disease by merely attending to its symptoms. You've got to address the deeper, less obvious processes that drive it.

Continuing with the medical analogy, suppose you've got the flu. Your head is pounding, you're coughing, and you're running a high fever. Well, what is it to have the flu? Ask your doctor, and they'll tell you that having the flu equals being infected with a flu virus. Headache, cough, and fever are all symptoms of the flu—they're *caused* by the flu, but they're not the flu itself. In fact, whenever you get the flu, there's a period during which you're ill before you develop those nasty symptoms. You don't yet know you're ill, because the indicators (symptoms) haven't yet appeared. Having the flu and knowing that you have the flu are two different things. You can't know you have the flu unless you really do have it, but you can have the flu without knowing that you do. On the flip side, the bare fact that you've got a headache, stuffy nose, and a fever doesn't *necessitate* that you have the flu. You could have all these symptoms and not have the flu. For instance, you might have a bad cold, or Weil's disease, or be infected with an adenovirus. However, even though the classic flu symptoms aren't foolproof, they're pretty good indicators that you've come down with the flu. When you have the symptoms and diagnose yourself as having the flu you're almost always right.

The same goes for the relationship between dehumanization and animalistic slurs or cruel and degrading treatment. These are often *caused* by dehumanizing attitudes, and we can use them to "diagnose" dehumanization, but they're not foolproof indicators. People can think of others as less than human without ever treating those others badly or describing them in animal-like ways (dehumanization can be very subtle, or even "asymptomatic"), and conversely, people can also treat others in cruel and degrading ways or call them animals without really thinking that they are subhuman beasts. But here, as is the case of physical illness, the symptoms are more or less reliable indicators that the psychological process of dehumanization is at work in the background, so they are important for making a diagnosis.

Why do I choose to think of dehumanization in this way rather than embracing some alternative? For one thing, I want to reserve the word "dehumanization" for something that isn't covered by other words. There's nothing to be gained by talking about "dehumanization" when words like "racism," "objectification," "othering," or "alienation" would serve just as well.

Also, the theory of dehumanization should be grounded in our best scientific knowledge. The main reason for studying dehumanization is to learn how to prevent or disable it, and to do that, we've got to understand how it works. And science is the only game in town for figuring out how things work. Because dehumanization concerns human attitudes and behavior, the go-to science is the science of psychology.

Further, I think that a good theory of dehumanization should be unified. By this I mean that it should zoom in on a specific phenomenon, rather than including lots of distinct things. The problem with big-tent concepts is that they don't give you a firm grasp on what it is that you're trying to understand. A theory of dehumanization will be most informative (and most useful) if it's focused on a single, distinctive phenomenon, rather than a plurality of loosely related ones.

Most of all, I think that a good theory of dehumanization should be consistent with those episodes in human history that are uncontestably examples of dehumanization. The Holocaust is one such. It would be strange, to say the least, to adopt a view of what dehumanization is that doesn't apply to the horrors of Auschwitz and Treblinka. Such a conception wouldn't merit being

taken seriously. The same can be said of a theory of dehumanization that's irrelevant to slavery, or to the anti-Black terrorism of
Jim Crow, or the horrors of colonialism, or many other examples.

To resist dehumanization effectively, you've got to know what
it is. You've got to be able to distinguish it from racism, misogyny,
xenophobia, or other forms of prejudice and oppression. To dehumanize others is to think of them not merely as inferior human
beings, but as subhuman creatures.

4 | HOLOCAUST

Rudolf Höss was the commandant of Auschwitz. He and his family lived in a lovely villa on the grounds of this sprawling factory of death. One day Höss's brother-in-law Fritz Hensel came to stay with them for several weeks. Decades later, the Israeli historian Tom Segev interviewed Hensel. This is what he wrote:

> Fritz Hensel . . . asked Höss once what the term *Untermensch* meant. They sat in the commandant's house, in the evening, over glasses of wine. Höss sighed. . . . "Look, you can see for yourself. They are not like you and me. They are different. They look different. They do not behave like human beings."[1]

The Holocaust is a prime example of dehumanization. Dehumanization of Jews was a central component of the Nazi program. And to date it represents the most explicit and thoroughly documented example of the dehumanization of a whole people.

Much of what we can learn from the Holocaust can be applied to other cases of dehumanization too, because dehumanization always conforms to more or less the same pattern. Of course, there are individual variations: the dehumanization of Black people by Whites is not the same as the dehumanization of Tutsis by Hutus, which is not the same as the dehumanization of Armenians by Turks. Each of these episodes must be understood against the background of different historical and cultural contexts, in response to different political forces, and each has features that are unique to it. But these differences make their striking similarities all the more significant, suggesting that dehumanizing states of mind are grounded in some very general features of human psychology. That's not to say that the dehumanizing impulse is innate, or that it was installed in our minds by evolution, or that these tendencies can never be overcome. But it *is* to say that we so easily slip into thinking of others as less than human in part because of how the human mind is configured.

The Holocaust had deep roots in Christian anti-Semitism. For centuries, Jews were the only religious minority that was permitted to exist in Europe and its colonies, albeit in a state of subjugation. When missionaries or conquerors encountered other sorts of non-Christians, they either converted them, often by force, or simply slaughtered them, but the suffering inflicted on Jews was a specific and sustained form of cruelty, marked by accusations of infanticide, pogroms, expulsions, and physical and cultural segregation. Its history is too long to retell here.

There's no better example of the dehumanization of Jews in the pre-Nazi, Christian European past than the ubiquitous image of the *Judensau* (the "Jew-pig"). From the twelfth century onward, many churches and public buildings, mainly in Germany but also elsewhere in Europe, were adorned with images of Jews sucking milk from a sow's teats, as though they were piglets, or inspecting a pig's anus, or sometimes it was a composite beast with a Jew's head on a pig's body. Later on, in an era of more widespread literacy, the Jew-pig image circulated in pamphlets and broadsides, accompanied by text that described Jews as dirty swine that guzzle filth. Later still, in the early decades of the twentieth century, the expression "Jew-pig" survived as an anti-Semitic slur that was quickly appropriated and proliferated by Nazi ideologues. It was around the same time that the Nazis adopted and somewhat transformed a traditional German proverb that pointed unambiguously to the sub-humanity of Jewish people: "Yes the Jew has the form of the human. However, it lacks the human's inner being." The distinguished and influential German jurist and political philosopher Carl Schmitt turned this racist saying into a toxic political slogan: "Not every being with a human face is human." Jews were considered as something like swine with human faces. They merely appeared to be human, but were nothing but filthy animals beneath the surface, and were compared to an infestation of rats in the notorious propaganda film *The Eternal Jew*.

The racialization of Jews laid the foundation for their dehumanization. To the Nazis, as well as to many other Europeans, Jews were a *racial* minority. The 1935 Nuremberg laws, which were passed to disenfranchise Jewish citizens of the German state, and which were inspired by the Jim Crow laws of the American South, were explicitly *race laws*. This was crucial, because Hitler and his followers were obsessed with the role of race in human affairs. They interpreted human history as the struggle for dominance between races, and believed that the highest moral good was to subordinate one's narrow self-interest to the greater well-being of the race. The Nordic or Aryan race was seen as the highest form of life, while the Jewish race—a race of *Untermenschen* or "subhumans"—was its implacable enemy.

There is a lesson to be taken from this. Dehumanization is enmeshed with beliefs about race. Groups of people who've been dehumanized are almost always first treated as racially alien. This might seem strange, given my definition of dehumanization. How can it be that members of a race—a *human* race—are thought to be *subhuman*? Isn't this a blatant contradiction?

Looking closely at Nazi propaganda dispels the appearance of contradiction. In 1942, the SS published a booklet entitled *The Subhuman*, which was all about Jews as less-than-human creatures. One of its main points was that although Jews look human, they aren't really human. As the text puts it, "Although it has features similar to a human, the subhuman is lower on the spiritual and psychological scale than any animal. Not all of those who appear human are in fact so. Woe to him that forgets it!" These sentences convey the idea that there's a difference between what Jews appear to be and what they really are. Although Jews look human, they're really only ostensibly human. They consist of a subhuman core that's concealed beneath a veneer of humanness. Jews and other dehumanized groups were not imagined as a human race of subhumans, but rather as a race of subhumans disguised as a human race.

Imagine a world where there are nonhuman creatures that are disguised as humans. This would be strange and disturbing. And it would be even stranger and more disturbing if you believed that these pseudo-humans were malevolent entities bent on destroying true humans and everything that they've achieved. But that's exactly what committed Nazis believed about Jews, as is very clear from another passage from *The Subhuman*:

This subhuman hates all that is created by man. This subhuman
has always hated man, and always secretly sought to bring about
his downfall. . . . The subhuman thrives in chaos and darkness,
he is frightened by the light. These subhuman creatures dwell
in the cesspools, and swamps, preferring a hell on earth, to the
light of the sun. . . . The subhuman hordes would stop at nothing
in their bid to overthrow the world of light and knowledge, to
bring an apocalypse to all human progress and achievement.
Their only goal is to make a desert wasteland of any nation or
race that shines with creativity, goodness, and beauty.

Just for a moment, ignore the historical context of this material. Forget that it's Nazi propaganda and just concentrate on the
themes, as though it were a description of the plot of a movie. The
story goes something like this. There is a horde of subhuman entities that pass themselves off as human beings. Although these evil
and repulsive entities aren't human, they aren't mere animals either. They're something altogether different—something demonic
or monstrous. Their mission is to take over the world and to destroy the human race.

There's no mystery about what kind of movie this would be.
It would be a horror movie. Perhaps one about a zombie apocalypse, or a plague of vampires, or hostile aliens from another world
that morph themselves into human form. Imagine yourself in
such a movie—or rather, imagine yourself in a world where this
is a nightmarish reality. That's the world that die-hard Nazis took
themselves to be inhabiting. They were terrified of those whom
they wished to exterminate. They conceived of the persecution of
Jews, culminating in the Holocaust, as an act of self-defense rather

than one of brutal aggression. They were so far detached from reality, so deeply absorbed in the fiction that Jews were not humans
like them, but something subhuman, and deadly, that they would
take any steps to exterminate them. This is the state of mind that
fosters genocide.

The Holocaust teaches us that when we are in the grip of a
dehumanizing mindset, we often see the dehumanized other
as toxic and frightening, resulting in what perpetrators see as
a life-and-death struggle against a deadly enemy. To combat dehumanization, it's crucial to understand that dehumanizers are
not just slinging animalistic metaphors at a vulnerable group.
Dehumanizers aren't just pretending. They sincerely believe that
those whom they persecute are less than human. And that's why
dehumanization has such immense destructive power.

5 | LYNCHING

The oppression of Black Americans during the century following the end of the American Civil War was enforced by
acts of terror that were so cruel that they defy comprehension.
Nearly five thousand Americans are known to have died at the
hands of lynch mobs during the nineteenth and twentieth centuries.[1] Four-fifths of them were Black. Many more went unrecorded.

Most Americans have an inaccurate view of what lynching
involved—one that they got from television and movies and that
minimizes the horror. The reality of lynching was far removed
from these sanitized representations. Racist lynchings weren't
merely extrajudicial executions. They typically included torture
and bodily mutilation, the breaking of bones, and the cutting off
of body parts of the living victim such as fingers, toes, and genitals, which were then put on display or kept as souvenirs. Often
the victim was burned alive at the climax of a lynching (which
is why Whites sometimes referred to lynchings as "barbecues"),
after which members of the crowd picked through the ashes for
memorabilia. Many lynchings were festive, public events that were
attended by hundreds or thousands of men, women, and children,

with special excursion trains laid on to transport spectators to the scene of the torture and professional photographers on hand to turn their fond memories into postcards.

Here's just one example. One of many, many others.

Claude Neal was a twenty-three-year-old Black man who lived in Marianna, on the Florida panhandle. On October 19, 1934, Neal was arrested and charged with the murder of a nineteen-year-old White woman. In the wee hours of October 26, a group of men burst into the jail where Neal was being held and took him away to a remote spot in the North Florida pine woods, where they tortured and killed him. The NAACP sent a representative named Howard Kester to Marianna to investigate. Perhaps because he was a White man, Kester found a member of the mob who was willing to tell him what happened that night. Here's an excerpt from Kester's report:

"After taking the nigger to the woods about four miles from Greenwood, they cut off his penis. He was made to eat it. Then they cut off his testicles and made him eat them and say he liked it. . . . Then they sliced his sides and stomach with knives and every now and then somebody would cut off a finger or two. Red hot irons were used on the nigger to burn him from top to bottom." From time to time during the torture a rope would be tied around Neal's neck and he was pulled up over a limb and held there until he almost choked to death when he would be let down and the torture begun all over again. After several hours of this unspeakable torture, "they decided just to kill him."[2]

The horrors inflicted on this young man were not exceptional. They were typical of what the Black victims of lynch mobs were subjected to. And this naturally raises the question of what made these acts possible. I'm not asking what made them legally possible—it was the persistent refusal of Congress to make lynching a federal offense, the failure of state governments to intervene, and the refusal of the courts to prosecute lynchers (even when the identity of gang leaders was well known, the victim was said to have been killed "at the hands of persons unknown"). I'm asking the deeper and more difficult question of what made these acts psychologically possible. It's crucial to ask that question because the men who tortured and killed Claude Neal, as well as many thousands of others who perpetrated these crimes, were ordinary people. They weren't sociopaths. Many were family men, churchgoers, and pillars of their communities. And the grotesque spectacles of torture and execution were enjoyed by their wives and children. What was it, psychologically speaking, that empowered them to do these things and the spectators to relish them?

Part of the answer lies in dehumanizing beliefs that many Whites held about Black people—especially Black men. One need only look at the descriptions in the literature and newspapers of the day to see what the Black image in the White mind amounted to. Newspapers commonly described the Black men who were the victims of lynching as less than human beings. They were "brutes," "beasts," "monsters," or "fiends." The search for Black men accused of crimes had echoes of a hunting expedition. The victim was pursued in a manhunt, and was often tracked by hunting dogs. Once caught and killed, the kill was memorialized with a trophy photograph of the hunter proudly posing beside his quarry.

Representations of Black people as subhuman animals weren't confined to the popular press. They also bore the stamp of academic authority. The major nineteenth-century American scientific text on race was *Types of Mankind*—a massive tome first published in 1854 that propounded, among other things, that the races are really separate species. Belief in the subhumanity of Blacks was entrenched and pervasive among the White intellectual elites, as the great African American sociologist W. E. B. Du Bois observed in 1899:

> [The] widening of the idea of common humanity is of slow growth and today but dimly realized. We grant full citizenship in the World Commonwealth to the "Anglo-Saxon" (whatever that may mean), the Teuton and Latin; then with just a shade of reluctance, we extend it to the Celt and Slav. We half deny it to the yellow races of Asia, admit the brown Indians to an ante-room only on the strength of an undeniable past; but with the Negroes of Africa we come to a full stop, and in its heart the civilized world denies that these come within the pale of nineteenth-century Humanity.[3]

Have things changed since then? Yes, of course they have. There are no longer public lynchings or segregated public facilities. And the overwhelming majority of serious scientists deny the biological reality of race, and would scoff at the idea that Black people and White people are really separate species with no common evolutionary ancestors. However, things haven't changed nearly as much as many White people would like to believe. We Americans have still not confronted our national crimes—the genocide of

Native Americans and the enslavement and oppression of African Americans—perhaps because we have never been compelled to do so. Massive racialized disparities in income, wealth, health, and mortality remain. Black, Latinx, and Native people are still assigned to the lowest rungs of a racial hierarchy, and White America has by and large refused to consider—much less to implement—reparations to the victims of its long history of state-sponsored injustice.

To combat dehumanization, it's vital to get to know our past in all of its horror and tragedy, because doing so punctures the self-serving illusion of American exceptionalism. A public that is educated about its own dark history will not only have to admit that that they—that is, we—are capable of the very worst, but also will become more open to recognizing the persistence and rebirth of dehumanizing attitudes in the present.

6 | HOW WE DO RACE

As the last two chapters have shown, dehumanization is bound up with racism. But to understand why that's so important, we've got to take a closer look at what it means to conceive of a group of people as belonging to a race.

Beliefs about race seep into almost every corner of our lives. As legal scholar Dorothy Roberts points out, "Race determines which church most Americans attend, where they buy a house, what persons they choose to marry, whom they vote for, and the music that they listen to. Race is evident in the color of inner-city and sub-urban schools, prison populations, the US Senate, and Fortune 500 boardrooms."[1] But despite its pervasiveness and significance, and its implications for human lives, few of us ever pause to consider what, exactly, race is supposed to be. What are we talking about when we talk about race? Is it something about people's appearance? Or is it something deeper?

In this chapter, I'm going to tease out the core elements of the *ordinary conception of race*. This isn't a fancy scientific or philosophical definition of race (I'll talk a bit about those later on). It's the view of race that most of us just slip into when going about the everyday business of life. It's a conception that we take so thoroughly for granted that we don't even question it. But to understand dehumanization we've got to open that Pandora's box, because beliefs about race lie at the heart of the dehumanizing process.

First, a few words of caution. Race is very easy to misunderstand, for a couple of reasons. One is that we tend to overgeneralize the racial assumptions that are prevalent here and now. That's a mistake because the particulars of racial categorization are often different at different times and at different places. To get a grasp of the ordinary conception of race it's important to abstract away from the details and identify the basic *template* of racial thinking, which remains more or less constant across time and space.

Part of this involves letting go of the tendency to equate race with skin color. Americans tend to think of race as very closely connected with skin color—so much so that "race" and "skin color" are often used interchangeably. But this connection doesn't apply across the board. European Jews had skin that was every bit as pale as that of the Germans who persecuted them, but this didn't prevent the Nazis (and others) from considering them as a separate race. The Tutsi and Hutu—victims and persecutors in the Rwanda genocide—were labeled as different races by the Belgian colonial administration, and came to think of themselves as such. But this wasn't based upon differences in skin color. And it's common for people in Japan to think of Korean and Chinese people as racially alien without any reference to the color of their skin. Color is an important marker of race in the Americas and Europe for historical reasons involving colonialism and slavery, but there can be racial difference without color difference, and color difference without racial difference.

Finally, it's crucial not to be hung up on the *word* "race." Some scholars tie the concept of race very closely to the word "race," and they have the idea that nobody had a concept of race prior to the use of the word in its modern sense. This simply isn't true. You don't need the word "race" to have the concept of race any more than you need the word "porcupine" to have the concept of porcupines. (I'm pretty sure that our prehistoric ancestors had no difficulty thinking about porcupines long before they had a name for them.) In fact, once the concept of race gets unpacked, you see that people use words like "ethnicity," "culture," and even sometimes "religion" and "nationality" to talk about race without even realizing that's what they're doing.

Enough preliminaries. Let's get on with it.

Part of the ordinary conception of race is what philosophers call *natural kinds*. Natural kinds are the sorts of things that exist "out there" in nature rather than being human creations. Chemical elements, biological species, and the elementary particles described by physicists are natural kinds. In contrast, invented kinds are artifacts produced by human beings (and possibly other intelligent life forms). Makes and models of cars, Thursdays, and dollars are all invented kinds. If human beings didn't exist, cars, Thursdays, and dollars wouldn't exist either, but elements, species, and subatomic particles would still be there. Some invented kinds are real and others are fictional. This book was invented, but it's perfectly real. But hobbits—which were also invented—are purely fictional.

When it comes to kinds of human beings, we think of some of these as natural and some as invented. For instance, it's widely believed that males and females are natural kinds, and disputes about the possibility of changing one's gender are often driven by clashing assumptions about whether men and women are natural kinds or invented ones. Whatever your particular stance is, we can all agree that there are lots more invented human kinds than there are natural ones. Some of these are real: professional categories such as "teacher" and "doctor" are examples. Others, such as witches and zombies, are fictional. (I don't deny that there are people who believe themselves to be witches, and there might even be a few who believe that they're zombies, but that's beside the point.)

So, where does race fit in to this conceptual landscape? Are races natural kinds or are they invented kinds? And if they're invented kinds, are they real or are they fictional ones?

People ordinarily think of races as natural kinds. They think that a person's race is something that's objectively true of them, rather than being merely a matter of how other people categorize them. A person's race is thought to be something that makes them the person that they are—something that's deep and unalterable, and which gets passed down, biologically, from parents to their children.

Scholars who study race call this the idea of *racial essentialism*. The idea that things have essences is crucial for understanding dehumanization, and I'll have more to say about it in chapter nine. But for now, the key point is that the essence of a thing is supposed to be something about it—something that's deep and unobservable—that makes it belong to a natural kind. Chemistry is one of the few domains where essentialism earns its keep. Hydrogen is made out of atoms that have only one proton. That's why hydrogen is assigned the atomic number 1. All hydrogen atoms have the atomic number 1, and nothing that's not hydrogen has that atomic number. It would be impossible for a hydrogen atom to have two protons, because an atom with two protons is a helium atom not a hydrogen atom. So, we can say that the essence of hydrogen is located in the microstructure of the hydrogen atom. It's the microstructure of chemical elements that determines how they behave and how they appear to us. Because of its microstructure—its essence—hydrogen behaves very differently from gold, which has seventy-nine protons. These microscopic differences explain why you can have a ring that's made out of gold but you can't have one that's made out of hydrogen. This points to a very general feature of essentialistic thinking: the principle that *the essence of a thing is what determines its outer properties*. This way of thinking really does apply in chemistry. All of the features of gold—its weight, its conductivity, its melting point, and so on—are outcomes of its essential microstructure.

Racial thinking follows much the same pattern. According to the ordinary conception of race, there's some deep defining property for each race—the racial equivalent to an atomic number—that's located "inside" a person, and which all and only individuals who belong to that race possess. This racial essence is said to determine the more superficial, observable characteristics of members of that race: how they look, how they think, and how they behave.

The theory of essences doesn't make any scientific sense when it's applied to races. As a matter of biological fact, there just isn't a racial equivalent of an atomic number. Races don't really have essences. We just imagine that they do. But despite its falsity, racial essentialism maintains a fierce grip on the human imagination. Most people find themselves buying into it. They operate with the implicit or explicit assumption that there are deep biological differences between people who are said to belong to different races. And even those who really do know better—people like biologists and philosophers—can have a hard time keeping themselves from slipping into the essentialist mindset.

Let's look a little closer at the connection between a person's race and their appearance. According to the ordinary conception of race, it's the unfolding of people's racial essence—its expression in their bodily form and psychological character—that causes them to look and behave in ways that are typical of their race. In this book, I'm using the word "appearance" to cover the whole gamut of observable characteristics, including their behavior. So, according to the ordinary concept, it's this process of unfolding that determines the race-specific aspects of a person's appearance, and that's why we're normally able to infer people's race from their appearance. If they have certain physical features that are typically associated with a certain race, we assume that they belong to that race. In light of what I've already said about racial essences, this can only mean that a person's appearance is assumed to be a *reliable sign* of their race.

According to the ordinary conception, a person's race is determined by something that's inside them that can never be perceived *directly*. The racial essence (which, I'll remind you, is supposed to be what *makes it the case* that a person is a person of a certain race) is by definition unobservable. This means that when we classify people racially, it's always a kind of conjecture. A person's appearance is taken to be an indication of their race, just as, for example, the color of a tomato is supposed to be an indication of its ripeness. The bright red color of the tomato *tells us* that it is ripe—it's a symptom of ripeness rather than the ripeness itself. And although the red color is very often a reliable indicator of ripeness, this isn't always the case. Some varieties of tomato turn yellow or orange or even purple, rather than red, when they're ripe. Similarly, the ordinary conception of race allows that a person's appearance may be deceptive. Their true racial identity may not match up with their appearance.

There's a compelling example of such a mismatch in Lillian Smith's memoir *Killers of the Dream*. Lillian Smith was a novelist and Civil Rights activist who grew up in the Deep South at around the turn of the twentieth century. In one of the chapters, Smith (who was a White woman) describes a formative experience from her childhood. A very fair-skinned girl was spotted in the Black section of her segregated town. On hearing of this, a group of White women jumped to the conclusion that the little girl had been kidnapped by the Black couple that she was living with, so they told the local sheriff, who took the child into custody and then fostered her with Lillian's family.

The girl, whose name was Janie, quickly became part of the Smith household. She and Lillian became fast friends, until an unexpected phone call from an African American orphanage shattered their relationship. The caller explained that, despite appearances, Janie was in fact a *Black* child who had been adopted rather than abducted by the Black couple she had been living with. Lillian recalled the following:

In a little while my mother called my sister and me into her bedroom and told us that in the morning Janie would return to Colored Town. . . . And then I found it possible to say, "Why is she leaving? . . ."

"Because," mother said gently, "Janie is a little colored girl."

"But she's white!"

"We were mistaken. She is colored."

"But she looks—"

"She is colored. Please don't argue!"[2]

That a person can look White but be categorized as Black seems odd, but it's perfectly in line with the ordinary conception of race. That's because the ordinary conception of race is actually a *theory* of race. It's what's called a "folk theory" rather than a fancy scientific or philosophical one. The purpose of any theory—whether it's a folk theory or a scientific one—is to explain some aspect of our world. Scientific theories make sense of observable things by postulating the existence of unobservable things that explain them. For example, chemists make sense of the properties of hydrogen by citing its microstructure. In the same way, the folk theory of race explains something that's observable by positing the existence of something that's unobservable. We observe that people come in different physical packages and behave in a wealth of different ways, and we use the idea of hidden racial essences to explain this observable diversity. But although we can see diversity, we can't *see* race.

Dividing human beings into races—into "our kind" and "their kind"—is the first step on the road to dehumanizing them. We first set them apart as a fundamentally different kind of human being—we treat them as a separate race—and only later transmute them into subhuman creatures fit to be exterminated or enslaved. Bad ideas about race are worth combatting all on their own, but all the more so because conceiving of people as racially other so easily morphs into dehumanizing them.

7 | RACISM

In 2015, a young White man named Dylann Roof walked into a church in Charleston, South Carolina, and gunned down nine Black Americans. In a powerful article about this massacre published in *The New Republic*, Rebecca Traister got to the heart of the matter when she stated that Roof "provided the United States with the latest installment of a history lesson we adamantly refuse to learn: that our racist past is not past." She continued:

> It is present. It is unending. It is, in many ways that we seem congenitally unable to acknowledge, fundamentally unchanged. . . . It is a terrible reality. The cold reality of our country right now. We are not post–civil rights. We are not post-race. We are not better than we were. We do not inhabit a world in which stray instances of violence might recall a distant and shameful history. This shame is a flood that has never abated.[1]

Racism will be with us as long as the notion of race remains intact. And as long as racism persists, dehumanization is just around the corner. I'm aware that this is likely to sound strange or even incredible to you, because it's commonly believed that ideas about race can be detached from racist attitudes, and that we can accept that there are races without buying into racism. I don't agree with this. I think it's worse than wrong, because it prevents us from coming to grips with the continuing problem of racism.

The first thing that we need to look into is exactly what racism is. "Racism" is a problematic word because, like "dehumanization," it has come to mean so many different things. One view of racism, one that's probably the most common among the general public, is that racism is race-based hatred. That's why in the mass media racism is often described as "hate," and racist speech is often called "hate speech." This concept doesn't sit well with what we want the concept of racism to do. Someone who isn't *hostile* to others because of their race, but who believes that they are inferior to his own kind is surely a racist. And what about someone who views others through the prism of racial stereotypes, even if those are positive (for example, someone who assumes that Asians are naturally good at math, or Blacks have a talent for basketball in their blood)? Shouldn't this person be considered a racist too?

Another idea is that racism is just indifference to the well-being of those who are deemed to be racially "other." This is obviously incompatible with hating people because of their race (you can't hate someone and also be indifferent to them). And it's not the same thing as looking down on them or believing that they are inherently inferior (you can simply not care about someone without thinking of them as lesser beings). Other approaches to racism don't emphasize what goes on in people's heads, but focus instead on what people actually do out in the world. On this view, if you behave in ways that selectively harm or disadvantage people of a certain race, then you are a racist, irrespective of your feelings, attitudes, or intentions. And then there's structural racism—the idea that institutions and organizations are structured in ways that empower certain racialized groups and disempower others.

As you can see, the meaning of "racism" is all over the map. And this broad range of meanings makes it all too easy for people who are accused of racism to reject the charge, sometimes in good faith and sometimes in bad. Because of this ambiguity surrounding the word, it would be far more useful just to spell out what we mean— for example, to say of a person that they hate members of other races, or have contempt for them, or fear them, or have disparaging beliefs about them.

If I had my way, I'd get rid of the word "racism" and replace it with more precise and explicit language. But the word "racism" isn't going to go away any time soon, so we should at least be explicit about what we mean by it. So here's what I mean by it. Racism is the belief that races exist and that some races are intrinsically superior to others. A person can be a racist, in this sense, even if they don't feel any hostility toward those whom they regard as their racial inferiors. American slaveowners were certainly racists, but they didn't *hate* their slaves, just as they didn't hate their livestock or their farming equipment. And on the flip side, it's also possible to hate the members of another race because they are members of that race without thereby being racist, because it's possible to hate other people without believing that you're superior to them.

Having put this definition of racism on the table, it's important to unpack it. The first question that needs to be addressed is what's meant by *racial superiority*. The answer isn't obvious, because there are lots of different ways that we can think of some people as superior to others. They might be superior in height, in strength, in beauty, in musical talent, in intelligence, and in many, many other ways. But none of these notions of superiority correspond to what racists have in mind when they judge themselves to be racially superior. To see why, consider intelligence. There no doubting that the Nazis regarded Jews as their racial inferiors. But they didn't see any contradiction between the view of Jews as their racial inferiors and the idea that Jews are diabolically intelligent. In fact, Adolf Eichmann, the man who managed the logistics of the Holocaust and who was a fanatical anti-Semite, believed that Jews were *more* intelligent than Aryans. He ranked Jews as superior to Germans *intellectually*, but ranked them as inferior to Germans with respect to their *humanity*.

Eichmann and other Nazis believed that Jews were inferior to Germans because they have less *intrinsic value* than Germans do. "Intrinsic value" is a philosophical term for the value that a thing has in and of itself, in contrast with its "instrumental value," which is the value that it has because of what it can get for you. If you marry someone for money, they have instrumental value for you, but if you marry them for love, you value them intrinsically. And money itself doesn't have any intrinsic value—its value lies entirely in what you can use it to get. It might get you something of intrinsic value (for instance, a great book, a trip abroad, a wonderful work of art).

Racists believe that each race has an intrinsic value. They think that the members of one race are objectively inferior or superior to the members of another *just because of their racial identity,* and therefore that each race can be assigned a rank on a hierarchy of value. Of course, it's possible for racists to think of some group as having little intrinsic value *as well* as being inferior in other ways. In fact, this is usually the case. But devaluing others on the basis of their race is what *makes* people racists.

The philosopher Kwame Anthony Appiah argues that there are two kinds of racism, which he calls "intrinsic" and "extrinsic" racism. Intrinsic racism is exactly what I call "racism"—the belief that others are inferior solely because they are members of a certain race. In contrast, the extrinsic racist thinks that members of a certain race are inferior because they have undesirable characteristics. A racist might look down on Black people just because they are Black (intrinsic racism) or she might regard Black people as inferior because she believes that they are inherently violent (extrinsic racism).

I don't think that this distinction goes to the root of the matter. That's because so-called extrinsic racism seems to always boil down to intrinsic racism in the final analysis. Consider the person who believes that Black people are inferior because they are violent. Suppose she's confronted with incontrovertible evidence that most Black people never commit a violent crime? She might just deny the facts, but the facts don't really matter, because her basic attitude is that although not every Black person actually behaves violently *they all have it in them to be violent.* She believes that violence is built into the Black racial essence, so Black people are inevitably, naturally, irredeemably violent, irrespective of whether that violence ever gets expressed in action. The propensity for savagery is always there, simmering away in the depths of their being, just waiting for an opportunity to burst out. Black people's crime is, in the words of historian Michael Berkowitz, the crime of their very existence.

There are many examples of this way of thinking in the history of racism. It's quite clearly expressed, for instance, in a speech by Heinrich Himmler to an assembly of SS officers in the Polish town of Posen. A recording of the speech has been preserved, so we can hear his inflection, as well as the laughter of members of his audience.

> I am talking about the evacuation of the Jews, the extermination of the Jewish people. It is one of those things that is easily said. "The Jewish people is being exterminated," every Party member will tell you, "perfectly clear, it's part of our plans, we're eliminating the Jews, exterminating them, a small matter."

And then he continues, his voice dripping with ridicule, "And then along they all come, all the 80 million upright Germans, and each one has his decent Jew. They say: all the others are swine, but here is a first-class Jew."[2] On the tape, you can hear members of the audience laugh at this bon mot. Why did it strike them as funny? I think it's because Himmler was heaping scorn on the idea that some of these Jewish "subhumans" (a term that he actually uses elsewhere in the speech) could be exceptions. Within the Nazi ideological framework, depravity was thought to be built into the Jewish nature, so the claim that there are "first-class" Jews would have struck his listeners as every bit as absurd as the claim that there are round squares.

The same attitude was expressed by the slogan "Nits make lice," which was used to justify the murder of Native American children, as well as by an old American proverb, "The Indian always returns to his blanket," which expressed the idea that Indians cannot be civilized, and will always revert to the savagery that's inherent to their nature. And it's the view expressed by many White Americans in the aftermath of the Civil War that, once liberated from slavery, Black men would yield to their darkest, most bestial urges.

The idea that some races are superior to others results in the idea of a racial hierarchy. In past centuries, mainstream European intellectuals—for example, the eighteenth-century philosopher Immanuel Kant—set all this out explicitly in writing. Unsurprisingly, given the human propensity for self-serving bias, these Enlightenment thinkers regarded White Europeans as the highest form of human life, and regarded all the other racial groups—Blacks, Native Americans, "Hottentots" (the indigenous Khoikhoi people of southern Africa), as well as others—as their inferiors. Assumptions about higher and lower races persist to this day. They're often explicitly stated by members of the alt-right and other extremist groups, and expressed less directly by ordinary citizens—or even those who consider themselves to be "woke." How could it be otherwise? The idea of race has notions of inferiority baked into it, and the crushing weight of centuries behind it. It's in the cultural air that we breathe and can't be switched off by dint of good intentions. That's not to say that beliefs about race are always destructive. In a racist society, the idea of race and racial pride can provide a sense of strength and solidarity for the oppressed. But this boon comes with a price—perpetuation of the circumstances that make such solidarity necessary. (And remember, the idea of race also provides a sense of strength and solidarity to the Nazis and White supremacists.)[3]

The ordinary concept of race is hierarchical because it's a product of conflict and domination. Racializing a group of people has the function of setting them apart, and placing them in a subordinate position (with the racializers setting themselves apart in a superior position). Racialized others are considered to be defective human beings whose true destiny is to be enslaved, exploited, or exterminated by the master race. This idea is an old one. We can find it in the writings of Aristotle, composed over two thousand years ago. Aristotle believed that there are two kinds (that is, two natural kinds) of people in the world: Greeks and Barbarians. He characterized Barbarians as "slaves by nature" and located them somewhere in between livestock and fully human beings (that is, Greek men), because they were not fully capable of rational thought. Aristotle believed that enslaving these people was good for them, because once enslaved they could then benefit from their proximity to the superior rationality of their Greek masters.

It goes without saying that the people whom Aristotle called "Barbarians" didn't consider themselves as Barbarians. They identified with the ethnic groups to which they belonged. They were Scythians, Persians, or Ethiopians, not "Barbarians." In ascribing a common nature to these people, by subsuming them under a single label and homogenizing them into a single natural kind, Aristotle defined them as enslaveable. By the criteria that I've presented in this chapter, Aristotle thought of Barbarians as a race, or as something very much like a race.

Many centuries later, Spanish colonists revived Aristotle's doctrine to justify enslaving the indigenous people of the New World. Aristotle's ideas about slavery were so ingrained that when the king of Spain called for a debate between the Dominican friar Bartolomé de Las Casas and the theologian Juan Ginés de Sepúlveda to settle the question, the conversation didn't address the question of whether slavery is ever morally permissible. Instead, it focused on the question of whether the Indians should be counted as natural slaves. Sepúlveda said "yes," and Las Casas said "no," but both took it for granted that there's nothing wrong about enslaving those who are slaves by nature.

Later on, English colonists took up the theory of natural slavery to justify enslaving Africans. There's no reason to think that the people of West Africa considered themselves as belonging to a single, homogeneous group prior to the transatlantic slave trade. Then as now, this region of the world was home to many diverse groups with varied languages, cultures, and physical appearances. If asked, they would have identified themselves as Igbo, Akan, Wolof, Fulani, or any number of other ethnicities rather than as "Black." It was Europeans who lumped them together as Black and negated their specific cultural identities. They subsumed these diverse people under racial labels in much the same way that Aristotle considered all non-Greeks to be Barbarians. And they did this because they had an investment in seeing all Black Africans as creatures of a similar sort—beings that they could enslave, abuse, and work to death on the plantations of the New World.

Like their ancient Greek predecessor, White slaveholders claimed to have done Africans a favor by enslaving them. In the United States, physicians gave this doctrine a medical twist. Physicians threw the weight of their scientific authority behind the claim that forcing Black people to perform hard physical labor was beneficial to them because it improved their frail cardiovascular system. And the doctors reasoned that because slavery is beneficial for Black people, any enslaved person who longed for freedom must be mentally ill. That's why the longing for escape from bondage was considered a psychiatric disorder, and was even given an impressively scientific-sounding name: *drapetomania*. If being enslaved was the proper condition of black people—the only condition in which they could lead fulfilling lives that are suited to their true nature—then anyone who wanted to run away was obviously delusional and needed to be brought back to their senses. The treatment for this condition was administered by the whip.

It's certainly racist to say, for example, that undocumented immigrants to the United States are freeloaders and criminals, but this derogatory way of talking stops short of dehumanizing them. As long as immigrants are characterized in this way, they're still seen as members of the extended human family, albeit members of an inferior kind. But when people are dehumanized they're extruded from the category of human altogether. They're not inferior people. They're not people at all. Racism ends and dehumanization begins at the boundary that separates human beings from the "lower" animals. Racism is the belief that some races consist of *lesser human beings*, but dehumanization is the belief that members of some races are *less than human beings*. Grasping this difference is crucial, because it throws light on why groups are almost always racialized before they're dehumanized, and why it is that racist attitudes so readily morph into dehumanizing ones. Dehumanization is racism on steroids.

8 | RACE SCIENCE

You might want to push back against what I've said. You might think that naïve, essentialistic ideas about the biology of race are bound to be wrong, but that science can give us a more accurate picture. In this chapter, I'll explain why science can't underwrite ideas about race.

Old, prescientific beliefs about the fabric of reality often evolve into newer, scientific ones. For example, medieval alchemists had some strange beliefs about physics and chemistry. They believed that everything in the universe was made from only four basic elements—earth, fire, air, and water—combined in various proportions, and that every metal has a "soul" that makes it the sort of metal that it is. But the alchemists' picture of the world didn't remain stagnant. Over the centuries, it gave birth to the science of chemistry, which replaced the old alchemical ideas with better ones. Eventually, scientists came to understand that there are ninety-eight naturally occurring chemical elements, rather than just four, and that metals don't have souls, but they have a physical microstructure, consisting of protons, neutrons, and electrons, that makes them what they are.

Scientists didn't *vindicate* alchemical ideas. They discarded them and replaced them with something new and better. That's why it would be ridiculous to ask, for example, which of the elements on the periodic table are earth, which are air, which are water, and which are fire, or to ask how protons and neutrons compose the souls of metals. There just isn't any relationship between these moribund alchemical notions and their present-day scientific counterparts. In philosophical jargon, the two frameworks are said to be *incommensurable*.

Not every case of scientific progress follows this same pattern. Sometimes the older concepts aren't just thrown away. They're refined. The theory of evolution is an example. Darwin's epoch-making book *On the Origin of Species* appeared in 1856. Later on, in the twentieth century, Darwinian theory was synthesized with the emerging science of genetics, giving rise to what's known as the "Modern Synthesis." The architects of the Modern Synthesis didn't trash Darwinian concepts such as natural selection and fitness: they refined and reconfigured them in light of new knowledge.

Could it be that although naïve ideas about race are coarsely hewn, crude, and deeply flawed, they can be refined into a scientifically acceptable conception? Or are these ideas about race like the four elements of antiquity, destined to be abandoned and replaced with something closer to the truth? If you're drawn to the first option, you're a "reconstructionist" about race, and if you opt for the second, you're what philosophers call an "eliminativist." As I hope to convince you, reconstructionism is a nonstarter. The ordinary notion of race can't be patched up so that it fits into a scientific picture of human diversity. Consequently, eliminativism is the only game in town.

Most people think that it's just *obvious* that race is real. That's because they're looking at human diversity through the lens of the concept of race and mistake the configuration of the lens for what they're observing through it. This isn't an unusual problem. If we look back in history, all sorts of what we now know to be falsehoods seemed to be obviously true at one time or another. For most people for most of human history, the idea that the earth is a sphere suspended in space would have seemed laughable. Likewise, the idea that races are human inventions seems absurd to many people. Taken as an argument, *"Race is obviously real! Just look around you!"* is on an intellectual par with *"The earth is obviously flat! Just look around you!"*

In sharp contrast with the person on the street, most scholars believe that races[1] are human inventions. They're more or less arbitrary divisions of the colorful tapestry of human variation. To see what's meant by this, let's return to the topic of skin color. Human skin color varies from the palest pale to the darkest ebony, and includes everything in between. Even though the skin-tone spectrum is continuous, and varies only very gradually from one geographical region to the next, we conventionally draw more or less sharp boundaries at several points on that continuum to demarcate white people from brown people and brown people from black people. The colors are perfectly natural, but the boundaries that are drawn between them are artificial. Where does white end and brown begin? The fact of the matter is that there's no fact of the matter. The line gets drawn where we *choose* to draw it (*if* we choose to draw it). The same principle applies to every other "racial" trait—hair texture, facial morphology, physique, and so on. It doesn't help to base race on geographical ancestry either, because the geographical lines associated with races are drawn every bit as arbitrarily as color lines are. The politically constructed region that we call "Europe" can be thought of as an aggregate of places rather than one big place. And if we do that, it's hard to see why it would make sense to say that a Norwegian and a Greek have ancestors from the *same place*, and that they're therefore members of the same race.

As I've explained, the idea of race relies on the idea that there's something about human beings that's deeper and more fundamental than mere appearance: the racial essence. In the past, the racial essence was supposed to be located in a person's blood, and passed down the "bloodline" from parents to their children and their children's children. That's why there are expressions like "full-blooded Indian" and the "one-drop rule," and it also explains why both German and American medical teams segregated blood by race during World War II. Because people imagined that a person's race was in their blood, any member of the dominant group risked contamination if they received blood from a member of an inferior race. If they received the wrong kind of blood, a White person might acquire Blackness, and an Aryan might become somewhat Jewish.

In hindsight, the idea that there's a racial essence that's carried in the blood was silly. No reasonably well-educated person nowadays believes that the races have different kinds of blood with the miraculous power of transforming the recipient's race into that of the donor. However, the idea that a person's race is in their blood has been replaced with the idea that race is in their DNA. This is a lot more sophisticated than the blood theory, but it's nevertheless incorrect.

Some people think that to deny that race is in the genes is tantamount to denying that human biological variation is under genetic control. But that's a huge mistake. It's obvious that there are genetic differences, on average, between racialized groups. The fact that some people have dark skin and some people have light skin is down to their genes, and the same is true of many other characteristics that are associated with racial differences. But accepting that genes matter for human variation is a far cry from the belief that there are distinctive genes that all and only members of races possess. The idea that there are sharp genetic discontinuities between the races just isn't consistent with what science tells us about patterns of human variation, but it's nevertheless a mainstay of the ordinary concept of race.

At least since Darwin, the term "race" has been used in biology to refer to what are known as subspecies. A subspecies is a variant within a species that's on its way to becoming a separate species. This subspeciation typically happens when members of a single species become geographically isolated. For example, there are three geographically separated subspecies of chimpanzees—the Western, Central, and Eastern varieties. Although they look very much alike, each of these groups is genetically distinct from the other two, and each can be regarded as an incipient species. So, why shouldn't we think of human races as subspecies of *Homo sapiens*? It's because they aren't different enough. There's a threshold of genetic difference that's required for any population of animals to be classified as a subspecies, and human groups don't come anywhere close to meeting it.

That's not the end of the story. Just because there aren't any human subspecies doesn't mean that races don't match up with real patterns of biological variation. There certainly are geographically linked patterns of biological variation in our species. But whether these patterns vindicate the ordinary conception of race depends on how we answer a deeper question: Do the patterns of genetic variation that geneticists have uncovered *support* ordinary notions of race or do they *replace* them? Is the ordinary notion of race like the alchemical notion of the souls of metals, or does it more resemble the modern evolutionary synthesis?

All human beings are practically identical at the genetic level. We all have the same genes, but there are different versions of some of them, and some of these have different effects from their counterparts. It's these variants—called *alleles*—that largely account for human biological diversity. So, for example, there are alleles that determine hair color. That one person has blond hair and another has black hair is down to the particular alleles that these two people have inherited from their parents. Not all alleles make a difference, as some genetic variations have identical effects. But here when I talk about alleles, I'm concerned with genetic variants with differential effects.

It's clear from what I've just said that if there are genetic differences between the races, these differences come down to differences in their alleles. Biologically uninformed people tend to jump to the conclusion that there are large genetic differences that mark off the races from one another, but this isn't true. In fact, most genetic variation is found *within* racialized groups rather than between them. It's only a small proportion of the already small proportion of genes that have difference-making alleles that vary between people of different races.

Still, a person might conclude that there's a subset of these alleles that *make* a person the race that they are—a genetic marker that's shared by every member of a race and by nobody else. But this isn't true either. There are certainly differences in the frequency of alleles between one group and another. A certain allele might be very common in one group but quite rare in another. But that's not to say that every person in the first group possesses the allele, and so it can't be true that the allele is what *makes* the members of that group belong to a certain race. (On the flip side, if even a small number of persons in the second group have the allele, then it can't be that the allele *defines* the first group's race.)

Those geneticists who continue to take race seriously focus on allele frequencies in human populations rather than alleles that are unique to populations. Allele frequencies pertain to statistical facts about whole populations, rather than facts about the genetic makeup of individuals. Using a computer program called STRUCTURE, geneticists can identify alleles that are relatively common in some groups of people and uncommon in others. Here's how it works: Scientists input lots of genetic data into the program, and then instruct it to partition the data into a specified number of groups (specified by the researcher), based on genetic similarity. The computer then executes the instruction. It sorts people into groups based on how their alleles cluster.

What does this have to do with race? When the computer is fed genetic data that are sampled from all over the world and it's instructed to partition these data into five clusters, the result corresponds to five geographical groups (Africa, Europe/Middle East/Central and South Asia, Oceania, and the Americas) that are associated with races. Some people think that this result vindicates our ordinary racial taxonomy.

There are several reasons why this is a mistake.

One (probably the least important one) is that the correlation between races and genetic clusters is quite rough. The cluster including Europe, the Middle East, and South and Central Asia just doesn't match up with any standard racial category, and the same is true of Oceania, which is home to a number of seemingly racially diverse groups. But the defender of races-as-clusters can fend off this criticism by saying that this lack of a perfect fit simply gives us grounds for revising, rather than discarding, the conventional racial groupings.

A second problem, one that's a lot weightier, has to do with the arbitrariness of dividing the data into *five* clusters. You could just as well tell the program to carve up the data into two clusters, or into twenty clusters, or two hundred clusters, or— if you had enough data—into two thousand clusters. If each of these divisions counts as a racial division, then there isn't any fixed number of races. And if only the fivefold divisions count as races, we need some explanation of why this is (there is no such explanation).

According to the ordinary concept of race, the division of the human family into races is a *privileged* division. That means that there's something special about racial categories that makes them more biologically significant than other ways of cutting the pie. But studies of genetic clustering don't show us this at all. Instead, they show that there are many different ways of dividing people into groups on the basis of genetic similarity, and they don't give us any reason to think that the fivefold division is especially important. Genetic clustering software allows us to discover statistical similarities and differences between human populations. That's all.

A third reason why genetic clustering can't justify the ordinary notion of race has to do with the difference between what's true of individuals and what's true of groups. Imagine that the average age of the residents of the street where you live is exactly forty-three years, five months, and three days. You'd get that number by adding up all their ages, and dividing this sum by the total number of people. That number—forty-three years, five months, and three days—might not be the age of any single *individual* living on your street, but it would tell you something about the whole *group* living on your street. Clustering software is like this. It identifies properties of whole populations, but not of individuals. There can be certain alleles that are common in a population without there being any individuals who have exactly those alleles, just like there might not be anyone living on your street whose age is the average age of people living on your street.

This is important, because according to the ordinary conception, race is considered to be a property of *individuals*. In other words, there's supposed to be something about individual human beings that makes it true that they're of one race or another. So, what makes a group of people collectively a race (the Black race, the Asian race, and so on), it's assumed, is the race of all the individuals who make it up. However, if we think of races as genetically clustered populations, then race is a property of whole groups rather than a property of the individuals who constitute the group. We could say that from the genetic perspective, individuals *belong* to races (again, assuming that we can equate races with population clusters) insofar as their allelic makeup approximates what's frequent in that population, whereas from the ordinary perspective, individuals *have* a race insofar as they possess certain racial properties.

Scientific studies of human genetic diversity don't vindicate the ordinary conception of race. Moreover, using the term "race" when discussing genetic diversity is both unnecessary and dangerously misleading. It's unnecessary because the term "race" doesn't add anything that's not already covered by terms like "population cluster." And its dangerously misleading, because it *seems* to bestow credibility on the ordinary conception of race, which, as I've explained, has racism built into it and which lays the groundwork for dehumanization. We should think of genetic clusters as an alternative to dividing people into races rather than a vindication of it.

The idea that there are human races is an illusion with a powerful grip on the human imagination. But it's an idea that we've got to oppose to combat dehumanization. This is hard to do, because there are deep features of our psychology that incline us to divide people into races, as we will see.

9 | ESSENCE

A Nazi SS officer gazes at a Jewish man being herded toward the gas chamber. What does he see? He sees what looks like a human being: a being with two legs, two arms, and hands equipped with opposable thumbs. He sees a being that wears clothes and speaks German; a being with hopes, aspirations, secrets, memories, and fears; a being that is terrified of his impending fate. In short, he sees a being who is very much like himself, his friends, and the members of his family. And yet, the SS officer does not see the Jewish man *as* a human being. He sees him as a human-looking subhuman.

It's hard to accept that one human being can gaze upon another and see that person as less than human—not in some fuzzy metaphorical sense, but as *literally subhuman*. It seems so incredible that it's tempting to grasp at some other explanation for the all too common descriptions of others as subhuman creatures. Couldn't it be that when Nazis claimed that Jews are subhumans, they meant it figuratively as a weapon for degrading and humiliating the Jewish enemy? Yes, of course, it could be that when the Nazis described Jews as *Untermenschen*, and when White lynch mobs described

Black men as predatory beasts, they were speaking figuratively. But this sort of skepticism comes cheap, and it's motivated by incredulity rather than evidence. True, dehumanization is remote from many people's everyday experience, especially those who are insulated from the most savage forms of racist abuse. But that doesn't have any bearing on the question of whether dehumanization, as I've described it, is real.

I think that in this case, as well as many others, our default position should be to take dehumanizers at their word. The fact that most of us think that dehumanization is something far removed from how we see others is irrelevant. Schizophrenic hallucinations are far removed from our everyday experience too, but that's no cause to doubt that they are frighteningly real. When a perpetrator of genocide says, in all seriousness, that he could not have butchered his neighbors if he had recognized them as human beings, we should listen to his testimony respectfully, and treat it with deadly seriousness.

The fact that people sometimes believe that other people who appear human are really less than human illustrates something important about how the human mind works. It shows that we don't think that merely looking human is what makes a being human. Instead think of humanness as something deeper that's "inside" of them—something more than the portions of the physical body that meet the eye.

Although this pattern of thinking might seem strange, it's actually quite familiar and comes to us very naturally. Our understanding of pretense and disguise is based on our ability to distinguish between what something seems to be on the surface and what it really is beneath surface appearances. This is a vital cognitive skill that often serves us well—for example, when we use it to recognize that others are deceiving us (or when we project a false impression in an attempt to deceive others). Think of salesmanship and politics. Think of hype. Think of attractive packaging that conceals defective goods or a dangerous product.

The distinction between how things seem and what they are also underpins the idea of racial passing. Recall that Janie was outwardly indistinguishable from a White girl, even though, according to the rules of the American racial taxonomy, she was definitely Black.

The notion that a person's appearance may give a false impression of their race is a problem for every racist regime. In such societies, members of the dominant group fear being infiltrated by those members of the oppressed group who look just like them. That such a fear exists implicitly challenges the whole idea of a racially stratified society, because it shows that the racial categorization doesn't correspond to real differences between people. This racial paranoia is most acute in situations where there aren't reliable-enough bodily markers of race. In the United States, the default assumption is that Black people have a distinctive appearance that makes them easily identifiable, even though very many people who are classified as Black, according to the norms used in the United States, are visually indistinguishable from those classified as White. In Nazi Germany, matters were less clear cut. Nazi functionaries who were charged with the task of segregating and later on exterminating Jews were confronted with the problem of distinguishing Jews from Aryans. Of course, there were many Semitic-looking Jews, but there were very many Jews who looked like Aryans—including tall, blond, blue-eyed ones like me. Even worse, there were olive-skinned, dark-haired Germans who could easily be mistaken for Jews.[1]

This explains why German citizens were required to document that they didn't have Jewish ancestors, why Hitler's government supported biomedical research aimed at finding something special about Jewish blood, and why Jews were marked out as racially alien by being forced to wear the yellow star. And it also explains the long-standing anti-Semitic belief that Jews are, by their very nature, masters of deception and disguise. The idea is clearly expressed in the infamous 1941 anti-Semitic documentary film *The Eternal Jew*, which was filmed in the Lodz ghetto in occupied Poland. At one point in the film the narrator intones (with ominous music playing in the background):

> The Jews alter their outward appearance. They leave their Polish haunts for the rich world. The hair, beard, skull-cap, and kaftan make the Eastern Jew recognizable to everyone. Should he remove them, only sharp-eyed people are able to recognize his racial origins. The essential trait of the Jew is that he always tries to hide his origin when among non-Jews.

The scene then switches to a row of bearded Jewish men, in traditional garb, facing the camera, shown one by one, while the narrator states, "A bunch of Polish Jews, still wearing kaftans." Next, the same men are shown clean-shaven, wearing suits and ties, while the voiceover explains, "And now in Western European clothes, prepared to infiltrate Western civilization."

Obviously, the concept of passing rests on the idea that a person's appearance isn't what makes them a member of a certain race. If you take the notion of passing seriously, you've got to believe that race is grounded in something deeper—something that doesn't meet the eye—a racial essence. The example of the relation between gold and fool's gold is a helpful analogy. Fool's good looks very much like gold, and is therefore very easy to mistake for gold. But gold and fool's gold are entirely different substances. Gold is a chemical element (number 79 in the periodic table), but fool's gold is a compound of iron and sulfur. Like a piece of gold and a piece of fool's gold, this kind of racialized thinking has it that two people may look like they're members of the same race, but they *really* belong to different races on the inside, where it matters. Dehumanization follows the same cognitive pattern that allows us to distinguish gold from fool's gold, and to embrace the idea that people can pass as members of a race that's not their own.

Both racial passing and dehumanization are grounded in what's called *psychological essentialism*: our seemingly irrepressible tendency to group things into natural kinds—for example, races or biological species—and to think that what makes any individual belong to one of these kinds is their possession of the essence of that kind. Just as races are supposed to have racial essences, species are supposed to have species essences. It's the species essence of an animal that's supposed to produce those aspects of its appearance that are typical of its kind. Take the example of cats. According to the essentialist mindset, what makes a cat a cat is its possession of an inner cattiness—the cat essence. And it's this cat essence that's supposed to manifest in the cat's body as typically catty traits, such as having retractable claws, tending to meow, being fond of milk, and so on. The cat essence shapes the cat's appearance through a process of development and growth.

There's also a "normative" dimension to essentialistic thinking. The essence of a thing is supposed to dictate the way that it's supposed to be (the way of being that's "natural" for it), and departures from this mark an individual out as deviant, pathological, or even monstrous. Returning to the feline example, the idea is that there's a way that cats are supposed to be, even though there are deviant cats that don't conform to type: cats with three rather than four legs, cats that don't meow, cats that dislike milk, and so on. These cats are seen as abnormal or defective, because their essence isn't fully realized in their appearance. In normal cases we can use the kind-typical characteristics to identify an animal as a cat, but in abnormal cases, the deviant appearance of an animal can lead us astray. A final and very important feature of essentialism is the idea that the essence of a thing is unchangeable and irrepressible. A cat *tends* toward cat-like behavior, which can be suppressed but can never be extinguished. Even though it might not be manifest, the inner cattiness is always poised to spring out. Once a cat, always a cat.

What I've just said about cats applies just as much to essentialist beliefs about races. Races are supposed to be natural human kinds with distinct racial essences. These essences are supposed to be located in our genes or blood, and are expressed in certain aspects of our bodily appearance, such as skin color, hair texture, and behavioral inclinations. Members of a race who look and act in a way that's thought to be typical or "natural" for members of that race are regarded as "true to their kind." But the ordinary conception allows that it's possible to belong to a race without displaying the stereotypical characteristics of that race, and no matter how ruthlessly their racial characteristics are hidden or suppressed, they inevitably tend to manifest themselves. And it's supposedly impossible for a person to change their race. The idea that race is ineradicable is captured in the title of Thomas Dixon's virulently racist novel *The Leopard's Spots* (the first book in his Ku Klux Klan trilogy),[2] set in the Reconstruction period after the American Civil War. The title is a reference to a sentence from the Book of Jeremiah: "Can the Ethiopian change his skin, or the leopard his spots?" and is meant to convey the idea that, having been freed from slavery, Black people would inevitably revert to savagery because that is an expression of their essential nature.

To a very great extent, the form of dehumanizing thinking has the same basic form as racial thinking does. When we dehumanize people, we think of them as apparently human on the outside, but essentially subhuman on the inside. From the dehumanizer's perspective, dehumanized people are *subhumans passing as humans*, because their humanness is only skin deep. Furthermore, dehumanized people are thought to be irredeemably subhuman. It is their permanent condition. Although these subhumans may be very good at mimicking true human beings, this is merely a façade and they are always on the verge of reverting to type. So, thinking that they are like "us," the *real* human beings, is a foolish and dangerous error.

We are all vulnerable to the dehumanizing impulse because we are equipped with a set of powerful psychological biases that make this possible. The tendency to essentialize kinds of living things helps us get along in the world, even though it's scientifically misleading. But it also produces states of mind that are immensely dangerous and toxic. Acknowledging your own tendency to essentialize, and remaining vigilant about combatting it, is a crucial step toward resisting dehumanization.

10 | FROM BARBADOS TO NAZI GERMANY

When Malcolm X stood up to give his first address as the founder of the Organization of Afro-American Unity, less than a year before his assassination in 1965, one of the themes that he emphasized was the vicious dehumanization of Black people in the United States. Here's a bit of what he said:

> Why, the man knew that as long as you and I thought we were somebody, he could never treat us like we were nobody. So he had to invent a system that would strip us of everything about us that we could use to prove we were somebody. And once he had stripped us of all human characteristics, stripped us of our language, stripped us of our history, stripped us of all cultural knowledge, and brought us down to the level of an animal—he then began to treat us like an animal, selling us from one plantation to another, selling us from one owner to another, breeding us like you breed cattle.[1]

Malcolm got it right. When one group of people dehumanizes another, they first think of them as members of an alien and inferior race: a lesser kind of human being. Racist denigration morphs into dehumanization when people are imagined to be not merely inferior, but to have a subhuman essence, and this promotes and legitimates their oppression in the eyes of their oppressors. This isn't the whole story of dehumanization. As you'll soon see, there's a lot more that needs to be said. But this is a good place to pause and consider a couple of examples. Although they're separated by hundreds of years and thousands of miles, they're uncannily similar, and they perfectly illustrate the intersection of hierarchy and essentialism that drives the dehumanizing process, often with catastrophic results.

Let's start in the seventeenth century. In the year 1665, a twenty-five-year-old clergyman named Morgan Godwyn, fresh out of Oxford University (where he had been a student of the philosopher John Locke) set sail for the colony of Virginia. His aim was to spread the gospel to enslaved Africans and Native Americans, who had been actively excluded from the Anglican Church. Godwyn soon came into conflict with the Virginia vestrymen—the wealthy elites who controlled the churches—and after an embattled five years set sail for the English colony of Barbados. By 1670, Barbados had become an economic powerhouse for the ever-expanding sugar industry. It was controlled by a ruthless, elite planter class, and it was a place where enslaved Africans were routinely worked to death, tortured, and mutilated. Godwyn spent ten years in Barbados before returning to England in 1680. The year that he returned, he published his most important work, an explosive little book entitled *The Negro's* [*sic*] *and Indians Advocate*.

Godwyn's book may be the first book ever written about the phenomenon of dehumanization. Of course, he didn't give a detailed analysis of its psychological dynamics (the science of psychology wouldn't be invented until more than two centuries later). But, on the basis of personal experience rather than third-hand reports or conjecture, he testified that White colonists thought of enslaved Africans as subhuman beasts. He detailed abuses inflicted on enslaved people, including the rape by White slaveholders, and condemned the perpetrators as "the Oppressor" and "the very dregs of the English Nation,"[2] who were motivated by their lust for profit and power to regard enslaved human beings as less than human.

As a devout Christian cleric, Godwyn's overarching concern was the colonists' practice of excluding Africans from the church. The exclusion was economically motivated. During the seventeenth century, the English were uncertain whether Christians could be legitimately enslaved. Colonists were therefore motivated to deny religious instruction to enslaved people, for fear that this would lead to their manumission. Godwyn makes it clear that this was an important motivation for dehumanizing Black people and Native Americans. Subhuman beasts can't possibly be Christians, and as non-Christians it was permissible to keep them in bondage. As Godwyn pithily put it in the title of a later publication, this was an example of "Trade Preferr'd before Religion."[3]

Looking closely at Godwyn's report, the core components of dehumanization are plain to see. Godwyn wrote near the beginning of the book that he had been told "privately (*and as it were in the dark*) . . . That the Negro's [*sic*], though in their Figure they carry some resemblances of Manhood, yet are indeed *no Men*."[4] Translating his seventeenth-century idiom into twenty-first-century English, Godwyn is telling his readers that Whites believed that although Black people appeared outwardly human, they were not in essence human beings. Later on, in the same text, he adds a bit more detail. Black slaves, he said, are "Unman'd and Unsoul'd" (in other words, dehumanized) and are "accounted and even ranked with *Brutes*" (relegated to a sub-human position in the hierarchy of nature). And in another work written several years earlier, and posthumously published in 1708, Godwyn stated in a similar vein that White colonists believed that Africans were "Creatures destitute of Souls, to be ranked among Brute Beasts, and treated accordingly."[5] As the possession of a soul was regarded as the essence of the human, any being lacking a soul was thereby excluded from the family of humanity. Godwyn held that the "unsouling" of enslaved Africans was used to justify the unimaginably cruel atrocities to which they were subjected.

Now, let's leave the horrors of Caribbean slavery behind and travel two hundred and fifty years and five thousand miles east to Germany, and then on to the Nazi extermination camps in Poland. In 1942, the Berlin publishing house of the SS—the elite paramilitary organization responsible for the sprawling network of concentration and slave labor camps, as well as the five extermination camps in Poland—produced the eye-catching pamphlet entitled *Der Untermensch* ("The Subhuman") that I briefly mentioned in chapter four.

Der Untermensch describes the Jewish race as a race of sub-human beings that are intent on destroying everything that's good and wholesome in the world: "Just as the night rises against the day, the light and dark are in eternal conflict. So too is the sub-human the greatest enemy of the dominant species on earth, mankind." The first page announces that Jews aren't human, despite appearing so.

> The subhuman is a biological creature, crafted by nature, which has hands, legs, eyes, and mouth, even the semblance of a brain. Nevertheless, this terrible creature is only a partial human being.

And the next paragraph states explicitly that their rank on nature's hierarchy is below humans:

> Although it has features similar to a human, the subhuman is lower on the spiritual and psychological scale than any human. . . . Not all of those who appear human are in fact so. Woe to him who forgets it![6]

Although hundreds of years and thousands of miles separate the two examples, the way that Jews are portrayed in *Der Untermensch* is uncannily similar to the descriptions in Godwyn's report. In both cases, the idea that a being can have a human appearance conjoined with a subhuman essence plays a major part. Of course, there are important differences between these two examples as well. Some of these are cultural (for instance, the Nazis didn't think that having a soul is what makes one human, so they didn't claim that Jews didn't have souls). But others have to do with the particular form of oppression that dehumanization facilitates. Black people in the Caribbean were dehumanized as part of their enslavement and they were therefore imagined as creatures akin to farm animals. Jews during the Third Reich were slated for extermination, and were compared to filthy vermin or diabolical monsters.

Looking at these episodes of dehumanization, we can see at work all the processes that I've described. Dehumanized groups are racialized and then attributed a subhuman essence that's said to lay underneath their human appearance. This makes it easier to perpetrate atrocities against them—to exploit, torture, or kill them.

11 | WHICH LIVES MATTER?

In August 2018, a truck skidded off the road in a rainstorm and capsized in the town of Brunswick, Maine, spilling its living cargo on the road. The truck was carrying lobsters to market—around seven thousand pounds of them, which, according to food safety regulations, had to then be destroyed. PETA (People for the Ethical Treatment of Animals) took up the slaughtered lobsters' cause. They proposed to erect a roadside memorial, inscribed with the words "In Memory of the Lobsters Who Suffered and Died at This Spot, August 2018, *Try Vegan*, PETA." I work in Maine and had a chance to speak to quite a few local people about the proposed lobster memorial. Most of them thought it was absurd.

We've seen that the idea that some kinds of beings are "higher" than others is crucial to understand both racism and dehumanization. The lives of those ranked higher seem to matter more than the lives of those ranked lower down. But to really understand this, we have to push the analysis deeper—we've got to figure out why the conviction that there are "higher" and "lower" kinds of beings is so stubbornly rooted in the human way of life.

Just twenty-five miles to the south of where the lobsters died, in the heart of the city of Portland, stands a bronze statue of the goddess of victory, ensconced on an impressive granite base. It honors the more than eight thousand men from Maine who lost their lives in the American Civil War. I don't know of anyone who thinks it silly to memorialize those who were killed in combat or died of disease during America's bloodiest conflict. Monuments like this one are treated with reverence rather than the disdain that greeted the proposed lobster memorial.

Why honor dead soldiers but not dead lobsters?

This question probably sounds strange, if not downright crazy. Isn't the answer obvious? It's because they're only lobsters, and people's lives matter a lot more than lobsters' lives. It's easy to accept that response, but not because it's backed up by any scientific fact. Biology doesn't—or at least shouldn't—endorse the notion that there are higher and lower forms of life. As soon as we start thinking of organisms in that way, we're leaving the scientific arena behind and moving into a very different territory.

Droves of philosophers have tried to justify the assumption of human superiority, without success. No matter what criterion you choose as the marker of our special status, it doesn't really work. A popular choice is rationality. According to this story, what makes humans special is the fact that we are reasoners, who possess autonomy and free will. But this isn't true of human infants—so are they more like lobsters than humans, and undeserving of our moral concern? And anyway, why should rationality set us above other animals? Even human corpses are supposed to be special, and treated with respect. But there isn't any morally significant difference between a dead human being and the carcass of a cow ready for butchery.

In ages past, the idea that there are higher and lower forms of life was tied to the concept known as the Great Chain of Being—the view that every natural kind is arranged on a grand, cosmic hierarchy. Traditionally, God—by definition, the infinitely perfect being—was placed at the top of the hierarchy. Human beings, who have traditionally regarded themselves as fashioned in God's image, placed themselves a little lower. Then, in descending order, came the nonhuman mammals, and the birds, fish, invertebrates, and so on, right down to inanimate matter. The occupants of each descending stratum were thought to have less value than all of those above them.

The hierarchical ideas about races that I discussed in chapter seven—notions that there are different kinds of human beings and that some of them are inherently superior to others—are part of this much bigger picture. Racial hierarchies are hierarchies *within* the human rank. During the eighteenth century, European scholars were quite explicit about this idea. They described White people as the highest form of human life, and other races lower down the scale. Those assigned to the bottommost rung—usually Africans or Native Americans—were pictured as bordering on the subhuman (just as Whites pictured themselves as closest to the divine).

Once it's clear that racial supremacist beliefs are part of a much larger framework, the relationship between race and dehumanization becomes a lot clearer. I've already explained how both racial thinking and dehumanizing thinking both rely on psychological essentialism. That's part of their connection. Now we can see how both also rely on the same sort of hierarchical thinking. Racialized people are typically thought of as lesser human beings. Because they are thought to possess an inferior racial essence, they are seen to be, by their very nature, at a lower level *within the rank of the human*. But dehumanized people are thought of as possessing the essence of a subhuman animal—an animal at a lower rank than the one that's occupied by humans on the hierarchy of nature. That's what makes them less than human rather than lesser humans.

Where does this way of looking at the world come from?

According to the philosopher Arthur O. Lovejoy, who wrote the classic book on the subject, the Great Chain of Being was based on ideas that were mined from the writings of Plato and Aristotle. Lovejoy says that it persisted through the Middle Ages, and faded away by the early nineteenth century as better, more scientific ideas about the origin of species took hold. But this story isn't correct, because it vastly underestimates the prevalence and persistence of the hierarchical idea. It wasn't just limited to Europe and the parts of the world that fell under European influence. It's been found all over the world. It's right there in the Book of Genesis, which describes how God grants humans domination over beasts of the field, and it's found in lots of other models of the universe, including ancient Chinese, South Asian Indian, African, and Aztec cosmologies, and, as I've pointed out, the belief that some forms of life are higher than others is deeply ingrained in how we think about nature. In theory, the Darwinian revolution should have demolished the belief that nature is arranged as a hierarchy (as Darwin wrote in one of his notebooks, "It is absurd to talk of one animal being higher than another"). But the Great Chain is still very much with us, and structures our thinking, behavior, and social policies. It's had so much staying power that even professional biologists, who, of all people, should know better, easily slip into the older, prescientific perspective. To prove this, the biologists Emanuele Rigato and Alessandro Minelli did a survey of more than sixty-seven thousand articles in major biological journals, including some of the most distinguished ones in the field, and, shockingly, found many references to "higher" and "lower" organisms in them. The distinguished journal *Molecular Biology and Evolution* turned out to be the worst offender, with 6.1 percent of the articles surveyed using hierarchical language.

All this raises two questions, the answers to which are vital for understanding how dehumanization works. First, if the idea of a human/subhuman dichotomy isn't just some metaphysical theory that came out of ancient Greek philosophy, then where did it come from? And second, given that the idea of a natural hierarchy is out of step with what our best science tells us about the relationships between living things, why do we have such a hard time letting go of it?

The first step to answering both of these questions is to recognize that the Great Chain of Being expresses a kind of psychological bias that makes it hard for us to think of the natural world in any other way. And even if we try, we've got to struggle against our gut-level intuitions that keep pulling us back the other way. Can you *really* bring yourself to think that a dandelion plant, or a goldfish, or a parrot, or even a chimpanzee, is of equal value to a human being? I doubt it. And if you can, you're a rare exception. For most of us—indeed, for almost all of us—some kinds of lives not only matter more than others but we believe that they also *should* matter more than others.

The idea that there's a hierarchy of nature—that there are natural kinds of beings that have greater intrinsic value than others—is essential to both racism and dehumanization. To combat racism, and the forms of dehumanization that flow from it, you've got to call this entire framework into question.

12 | THE ACT OF KILLING

We are an extraordinarily social species. In fact, there's no other mammal that comes anywhere near us in this regard. You might say that we possess an instinct for solidarity. Humans are this way because our very survival depends on being members of highly cooperative communities. It's been our condition for hundreds of thousands if not millions of years, and this applies just as much to hunter-gatherer bands dwelling in the Amazonian rainforest as it does to the residents of the sprawling urban metropolises of the so-called developed world. Our social way of life demands that we be exquisitely attuned to one another, and this has a significant impact on how we manage violence.

Like other social animals, humans inhibit severe forms of violence against members of their own community. For nonhuman animals, the community is limited to the local breeding group—the troop, colony, or pack. These inhibitions are needed, because social life can't possibly be sustained if the members of a group are at each other's throats. But these inhibitions against violence don't apply to strangers, who can be viciously attacked and literally torn to shreds without harming the social fabric.

Among nonhuman animals, the tendency to discriminate between insiders and outsiders, between "us" and "them," is a more or less automatic, instinctive response. But things go differently for us. Like other social mammals, we automatically recoil from performing acts of lethal violence against those whom we recognize as being part of our community. But in our case, violence-avoidance isn't automatically restricted to the *local* community. It extends to outsiders, to strangers, whom we cannot help but recognize as fellow human beings. This is a gut-level response to seeing others as human. It's not something that we can turn on or off at will. It happens to us rather than being something that we choose to do.

Our aversion to harming one another is in tension with a basic condition of animal life. Animals must kill, damage, or exploit other organisms in order to live. This is obviously true of predators that consume the flesh of others, but it's also true of parasites that drain their blood, and even gentle herbivores that kill and dismember plants. Human beings are no exception. We have a long history of killing other organisms.

It's impossible to know exactly how long we've been killing and eating other animals. It's very likely that some of our very early ancestors caught and ate small animals—insects, lizards, rodents, and the like—that were abundant, rich in protein, and easy to capture. They may have begun to eat the flesh of larger animals by scavenging kills made by large predators—mobbing and driving away the lions and hyenas with sticks and stones. This cooperative activity may have been a dress rehearsal for cooperative group hunting, which was well established over three million years ago. Whatever the details, it's clear that the organized killing of other species is a crucial part of the human story and may well have contributed to the evolution of our massive brains by supplying the precious calories needed to support this very expensive organ. Hunting was just the beginning. Once humans had abandoned their foraging way of life they domesticated animals, keeping herds for meat and milk, exploiting their labor, and using their hides to manufacture leather. And it's a straight line from there to the industrialized slaughter of modern factory farming.

The act of killing is monumentally important to human lives. The question of what kinds of beings are killable, and under what circumstances they may be killed, is perhaps the most basic of all moral questions. In all societies, it's permissible to take only certain kinds of lives and forbidden to take others. In some cases, there are sacred animals whose lives are protected, but whether or not this is the case, human beings are granted a privileged moral status, and are treated quite differently than most nonhuman organisms. That's not to say that killing humans is always forbidden. There are circumstances in which killing others is allowed or even mandatory (for example, in our own culture there's abortion, capital punishment, and killing in combat).

The special moral status that we accord to human beings is, I believe, bound up with our inhibitions against doing violence to them. Unlike other animals, we're driven to find reasons for our actions, and when we cannot find reasons we invent them. We then codify these reasons in systems of rules—rules that permit some actions and forbid others. So, we concoct justifications for why it's morally acceptable to do violence to some kinds of beings but not others.

One such justification, found in indigenous hunting cultures, is to deny that killing animals is really an act of violence. Animals supposedly choose to make themselves available to hunters and do this because they *want* to be killed. Philosopher T. J. Kasperbauer points out that, from this perspective, "animals are seen as willful participants who supposedly gain as much from the hunt as the hunters."[1]

This strange idea—which is backed by systems of belief about the supernatural realm—may have been widespread during our hunter-gatherer past. But it's certain that at some point in time, a different, more robust solution to the problem of killing took root, and according to this framework, we are free to kill or exploit those living things that are ranked beneath the human. We can kill cockroaches and lobsters and sheep and cattle in human cultures—the idea of a natural hierarchy that I discussed in chapter eleven—because they are "lower" in the grand scheme of things than we are. This ideological framework also had another advantage. It freed us up to kill and oppress our fellow human beings. With the hierarchical scheme firmly in place, we could subvert our inhibitions against doing violence to other people by representing those people as less than human.

The idea of the Great Chain of Being was a great invention, and like many other great inventions, it probably did not spring up at any one place at any one time, but arose independently in various far-flung cultures. The Chain is now thoroughly entrenched in our way of thinking, and our way of life, because it offers a powerful solution to the problem of killing. We all have to kill to live. Even vegans take the lives of vegetables.

The idea that nature is arranged as a hierarchy, and that our lives matter more than the lives of organisms lower down the chain, is an illusion. But because killing is a necessary condition for human life, it's an illusion that would be hard for us to do without. Because killing is mandatory for human survival, it's tempting to fall into the trap of hierarchical thinking, and to rationalize this bias with fancy philosophical arguments or religious beliefs. But to resist dehumanization, it's important to resist, and help others to resist, the fantasy that we are objectively "higher" than those plants and animals whose lives we take.

13 | MORALITY

I've said that our instinctive sociality accounts for powerful inhibitions against killing others that are intrinsic to human social life. This may sound strange to you, given the horrendous violence that litters our history. If human beings have inhibitions against killing, how come they manage to regularly prosecute wars and genocides?

Back in chapter three, I explained that there are many different views about exactly what dehumanization is—many *concepts* of dehumanization. Now I need to introduce a different wrinkle. There are also many views about how dehumanization works—many *theories* of dehumanization. Two people can have the same concept of dehumanization and yet have different theories of it. Put differently, two people might have exactly the same definition of what dehumanization is and yet have different and incompatible explanations of what causes it or what its function is.

Here's one theory of dehumanization, one that's popular but wrong: Some people think of dehumanization as the *failure* to recognize the humanity of others. Their story goes like this. We encounter people who are obviously very different from us—people who look differently, speak differently, dress differently, and so on, and then jump to the conclusion (based on these highly visible differences) that they belong to a different species. This account, if true, suggests that dehumanization should be fairly easy to eliminate. All that's needed is to convince dehumanizers that superficial differences aren't important and that they're committing a cognitive error when they think that the color of people's skin or the religion that they practice renders them so wholly other. The problem with this account is that dehumanization isn't some sort of oversight or blind spot. It is a motivated state of mind. It has a function—a raison d'etre. When Hutu genocidaires hunted down the Tutsi "cockroaches" and "snakes" in the Rwandan bush, it was not because they hadn't noticed that their victims were human beings. Hutu and Tutsi had lived and worked together for a very long time prior to the genocide. The genocidal killers viewed their victims as subhuman quarry precisely because they were motivated to exterminate them.

Another popular but incorrect theory is that when people conceive of other people as less than human, this is just an alibi to excuse their cruel and destructive acts. But the historical record shows that dehumanization has *motivational* force. It's not just a story that people tell to others to let themselves off the hook. It's an attitude that liberates ferocious aggression, and it only has this effect because perpetrators really do believe that they're battling subhumans. They often say so, sometimes quite explicitly, and I think that we should take them at their word.

Here's another misleading assumption. Academics who study dehumanization often claim that dehumanization promotes "moral disengagement"—a kind of distancing that casts others out from what the genocide scholar Helen Fein calls the "universe of moral obligation."[1] Moral disengagement is supposed to be what ties dehumanization to violence. The idea is that when we think of other human beings as creatures of an inferior rank, we value them less. Their lives and suffering count for less to us, and this makes it psychologically easier for us to treat them badly. This explanation is inaccurate. Dehumanization isn't *based* on differences in appearance, language, religion, and so on. In fact, dehumanizers typically seek out or invent differences to support their projects. As I've already mentioned, during the Nazi era, German Jews were often indistinguishable from other Germans. But that didn't matter to the Nazis. The regime tried to discover differences between Jewish and German blood, and had to make Jews visibly different by forcing them to wear the yellow star.

Another problem with this approach is that it misrepresents the character of our attitudes toward animals. Regarding a being as an animal isn't enough to make you want to harm it. That only happens if there's something *about* the animal that elicits this sort of response. Seeing a mosquito buzzing around your head will probably result in you trying to swat it, but noticing a group of sparrows on the lawn isn't likely to inspire you to go on a killing spree. If assigning a creature to a subhuman rank doesn't *in itself* motivate violence, then the bare fact of moral disengagement isn't enough to explain the connection between dehumanization and atrocity. That's why Fein insists that excluding others from the universe of moral obligation is necessary but not sufficient for genocidal violence. In Rwanda, the references to Tutsis as cockroaches and snakes represented them as dirty or dangerous subhuman beings—animals that *should* be killed.

Here's a better story. The desire to harm others leads to their dehumanization, rather than the other way around. It liberates antagonisms that are already there, simmering in the background and just waiting to burst out, or ratchets up violence that's already being done. On this view, dehumanization happens when one group of people sees some advantage in doing violence to another, but members of the first group can't square this with their moral values. Morally disengaging from the second group through thinking of them as less than human solves the problem, because it makes their actions ethically allowable. This certainly applies to the Rwanda genocide, where long-standing ethnic hostility set the stage for the outbreak of dehumanization and mayhem. In this case, as in many others, dehumanization helped transform preexisting antagonism into outright slaughter.

Although this account of how dehumanization works is more accurate than the first one that I mentioned, it's not exactly on target either. The reason why has to do with the notion that genocide promotes moral disengagement. "Moral disengagement" is a term from the vocabulary of social psychology. It refers to the process of disabling mechanisms of self-condemnation, so that a person doesn't feel guilt or shame when violating their own moral standards. But this phrase is misleading. To say that someone is morally disengaged from others implies that they're indifferent to the others' well-being. The attitude of dehumanizers toward those whom they dehumanize is anything but indifferent—it's typically *highly moralistic*. Take genocidal violence. It's almost always aimed at ridding the world of what the perpetrators believe to be some terrible evil. Consequently, those who enact even the most hideous genocidal atrocities often regard these acts as virtuous. As historian Claudia Koonz succinctly put it, "The road to Auschwitz was paved with righteousness."[2]

Rather than being morally disengaged, dehumanizers are usually highly—indeed, obsessively—morally engaged with the people whom they dehumanize, and it's this punitive and predatory form of moral engagement that stokes the fires of atrocity, fueled by moral fury.

Another reason why the concept of moral disengagement doesn't illuminate how dehumanization works concerns the important but frequently overlooked distinction between moral taboos and nonmoral inhibitions. It's not the case that we're reluctant to do violence to other human beings because we feel that it's *morally wrong* to do so, and that dehumanization unleashes violence because it liberates us from the burden of our moral scruples. When we see another being as human, we don't automatically think that harming them is immoral. In fact, many believe that humans are the only beings that sometimes *deserve* to be hurt or killed (for example, by beating, incarceration, or capital punishment), because they're the only beings who are morally responsible for their actions. Furthermore, even when a person believes that it's their moral duty to kill others (for example, in combat), it's often difficult for them to do the killing. They freeze, but not always because the act of killing conflicts with their deep moral beliefs. They freeze because of something quite different that's going on inside their minds—something that's nonmoral. The philosopher Richard Joyce describes this difference as the difference between *prohibitions* and *inhibitions*:

To do something because you *want* to do it is very different from doing it because you judge that you *ought* to do it. We can easily imagine a community of people all of whom have the same desires: they all want to live in peace and harmony and violence is unheard of. . . . However, there is no reason to think that there is a moral judgment in sight. These imaginary beings have *inhibitions* against killing, stealing, etc. They wouldn't dream of doing those things; they just don't want to do them. But we need not credit them with the conception of a *prohibition*: the idea that one shouldn't kill or steal because to do so is wrong.[3]

The resistance to performing acts of violence that I've been discussing in this book is an inhibition, not a prohibition. It isn't grounded in morality any more than social insects' chemically mediated inhibitions against intra-colony violence are. The fact that ants don't attack other members of their own colony isn't due to any moral considerations on their part. Ants don't have views about the difference between what's right and what's wrong; the restraint with which they treat their colony members is an automatic, modular, instinctive response to a chemical signal. Likewise, our inhibition against killing other human beings gets switched on automatically when we recognize another person as a human being. And when this mechanism gets overridden, dampened down, or switched off entirely—whether by dehumanization or some other process—this clears the way for viciously destructive moral fury.

The renowned political philosopher Hannah Arendt came close to articulating this in her book about the trial of Adolf Eichmann when she drew a contrast between "instinctive" (that is, automatic) recoiling from acts of lethal violence and disapproving of the same act on moral grounds. In a discussion of the *Einsatzgruppen*—the mobile killing units whose task it was to kill communists and Jews en masse in the wake of the German army's incursion into Poland and the Soviet Union—she remarked that "the problem was how to overcome not so much their conscience as the animal pity by which all normal men are affected in the presence of physical suffering."[4] This *was* a problem for Nazi mass murderers. Although they are portrayed as cold-hearted killers who followed orders robotically, or as diabolically sadistic, most of the men and women who participated in the genocide had to defy their aversion to inflicting harm on others. Thirty years after Arendt's comments, the historian Christopher Browning confirmed her insight. Here's his description of the aftermath of one unit's first mass shooting, the killing of around fifteen hundred Jews near the Polish village of Józefów:

> They ate little but drank heavily. . . . Major Trapp made the rounds, trying to console and reassure them, and again placing responsibility on higher authorities. But neither the drink nor Trapp's consolation could wash away the sense of shame and horror that pervaded the barracks. Trapp asked the men not to talk about it. . . . But repression during waking hours could not stop the nightmares.[5]

Because dehumanization isn't some sort of oversight, it can't be stopped or prevented by reminders that we're all human. Dehumanization is motivated by the desire to do violence to others, and has the function of disinhibiting our worst impulses.

That said, dehumanization is not, as many people claim, a mechanism of moral disengagement. The inhibitions that it undermines aren't moral ones, and the violence that it unleashes often has an intensely moralistic tone. Focusing on what's morally right will never put a stop to dehumanization, and well-meaning injunctions to see all members of our species as human beings won't get us there either. Instead, we must block the processes—both psychological and political—that subvert our automatic perception of the humanness of others.

14 | SELF-ENGINEERING

We humans have come to dominate the earth. But on the face of it, we're unlikely candidates for this position. Unlike other animals, we're not equipped with natural bodily weapons like sharp teeth and claws, but we made up for our deficit by chipping away at pieces of stone and hafting them to sticks to craft artificial weapons. Although our ancestors' bodies had no fur to protect them from the cold, they donned the fur of the animals that they hunted, and colonized land as far north as the Arctic Circle. Even the best human swimmers were no match for animals like seals and dolphins, but we more than compensated for our lack of natural ability by building boats to carry us across the seas. By the dawn of the twentieth century, we had even learned to fly. These are just a few of the ways in which we've extended our physical capacities, and there have been many, many more.

A big part of our success lies in developing technologies for enhancement, and transmitting them from one generation to the next. All sorts of components have to be in place and working in unison for this to happen. One is creative imagination. For humans to transcend their limitations they had to break out of the prison of the here-and-now by imagining unrealized possibilities. Another is instrumental thinking. To make real what's been imagined, they needed to work out the steps required to achieve the goal. And they require collective effort and intergenerational apprenticeships, which in turn depend on cooperation and social attunement. In other words, our relentless overcoming of limitations rests on the platform of human culture.

Culture does more than allow us to engineer material artifacts. It also allows us to engineer ourselves. Our knack for culture gives *Homo sapiens* vastly greater behavioral flexibility than is available to any other species, because it creates conditions that allow us to push back against some of the biological imperatives of human nature itself. Through culture, we can get ourselves to behave in ways that would otherwise be unavailable to us. Among these are ways that we have found to overcome our visceral aversion to performing acts of calculated, instrumental violence against our own kind. It's our feats of self-engineering that have made certain kinds of violence—by far, the most destructive kinds of violence—possible.

We developed these methods because we are able to see that such acts of violence can be materially rewarding. We can, and often do, picture a world in which we reap the benefits of exterminating or oppressing our neighbors, and we concoct plans for achieving these goals. But there's an obstacle that must be surmounted before we can execute such plans. The obstacle is an aspect of human nature itself: our hypersociality. Exquisitely attuned as we are to one another, we recognize that our intended victims are fellow human beings, and this triggers powerful inhibitions against doing

violence to them. We are drawn to harming others, but also burdened with a horror of spilling human blood.

This poses a problem, but not an insoluble one. And over
many thousands of years, human ingenuity found several ways of
solving it by learning how to selectively disable our inhibitions
against performing acts of atrocity. One method relies on material technology. We have weapons that make it possible for us
to kill at a distance, beginning, perhaps, with the stone-age atlatl
(spear-thrower) and longbow, and progressing to such engines of
destruction as today's sophisticated long-range firearms, bombs,
and guided missiles. These insulate the eyes and ears of killers from
the specific sights and sounds that trigger perceptions of humanness. They make killing easier, not just because they are efficient
weapons, but because they emotionally distance the killer from the
act of killing.

We use other practices to distance us from those we kill in psychological space without also distancing ourselves from them in
physical space. One approach, going back to prehistory, is to consume psychoactive drugs to create altered states of consciousness
that allow us to kill more easily. Many such substances have fit
the bill: cocaine, amphetamines, cannabis, opiates, hallucinogens,
and, of course, alcohol. "The presence of alcohol or drugs," writes
historian Edward B. Westermann, "has been noted in numerous
instances of atrocity throughout history." He continues:

> One of the most notorious examples of mass murder in the
> American West, for example, occurred at Sand Creek on
> November 29, 1864, when a group of Colorado Volunteers,
> many of them fueled by whiskey, initiated an unprovoked

attack on a settlement of Cheyenne Indians. The men butchered 105 women and children and 28 men. The massacre included an orgy of sexual mutilations, scalping, and the taking of body parts as trophies.[1]

Almost a century later, in 1955, Algerian rebels had used alcohol and a cannabis byproduct before massacring a group of *pied-noir*—not only killing many, but mutilating the bodies of women and children, Westermann notes. And as he also points out, alcohol and drugs were used with similar effect in Vietnam, and during the two world wars.

Another ancient method is to draw on spiritual practices to help us slaughter other human beings. Religious intoxication can be just as powerful a stimulant as chemical intoxication is, and can be combined with drugs to produce a frenzy of killing. Drugs merely destabilize our inhibitions, whereas ritual practices can be used to inspire and rationalize acts of violence and cruelty. There are many examples of this in the anthropological literature. For example, Simon Harrison gives a fascinating description of the pre-combat ritual practiced by the Avatip people of New Guinea:

When Avatip men went to war, and nowadays when they carry out a ritual, they say they take on a "different" and "bad" face. . . . It was in a similar, but more intense, state of magical potency that, in the past, men went on headhunting raids. Just before the fighters carried out the attack, the war-magicians bespelled them with the most powerful of all forms of Avatip war-magic. This magic could only be applied when the men were well away from the village because, once bespelled, they became capable of killing anyone, even, so men stress, their own wives and children. Men speak of war-magic as having induced in them a state of dissociation in which they became capable of extreme, indiscriminate violence, a kind of trance-state in which their only thoughts were of homicide. They speak of the aftermath of the fighting as a kind of re-awakening or recovery of their senses, of not even having perceived the enemy corpses until the magic was removed and their eyes became clear again.[2]

And even today's American soldiers listen to loud heavy metal and hip-hop music, and collectively chant the lyrics, as part of a pre-combat ritual that psyches them up for the horrors of combat.

More powerful than even drugs or ritual, dehumanization is a way of surmounting psychological barriers to committing acts of violence. By playing on our propensity for essentialistic and hierarchical thinking, and getting ourselves to think of certain others as dangerous or despicable subhumans, we discovered a way to empower ourselves to commit acts of cruelty and destruction. It's obvious that dehumanization is a problem, but it's also, paradoxically, a solution to a problem.

As hypersocial animals, we have strong inhibitions against harming our own kind, but we are also able to use our great big brains to recognize that doing harm to others can benefit those who are capable of overcoming their reluctance to performing acts of violence. Dehumanization is one way that we've found to disable our inhibitions, often with catastrophic consequences.

15 | IDEOLOGY

So far, I've concentrated on what goes on in people's heads when they dehumanize others. But that's only half the story. It's a mistake to analyze dehumanization as a purely psychological phenomenon—something that arises unbidden from within. *Dehumanization is a psychological response to political forces.* More specifically, dehumanizing beliefs are ideological beliefs. So, to understand how dehumanization works, and to resist it effectively, we've got to have a clear conception of ideology.

Explaining the nature of ideology isn't straightforward, because even though the concept is very popular, both inside and outside the academy, it has many different meanings. Sometimes it's used in a disparaging way, to say that a belief is more a person's political "agenda" then it is based on facts (this often gets framed as "ideology versus science"). At other times, or in other mouths, it's used in a neutral or even a positive way to refer to a set of beliefs to which a person is committed. And there are even finer distinctions made in the scholarly literatures of political science and philosophy. Because there are so many different views about what ideology amounts to, anyone discussing it needs to be explicit about what they mean.

One conception of ideology that's popular among philosophers these days is that *ideologies are beliefs that have the function of fostering oppression*. I think that this is a very useful notion of ideology, because it homes in on something important that we don't have another term for, so I've adopted it. But to be really clear about what ideology is, we've got to push the analysis further and look closely at the two core elements of the definition: the concepts of *oppression* and *function*.

"Oppression" is a word for situations in which one group of people gets some real or imagined benefit by subjugating another group of people. It's an intrinsically political concept, because it pertains to the distribution and deployment of power among whole groups of people rather than between individuals. People are never oppressed as individuals. They're oppressed because of their real or imagined group identity (race, gender, ethnicity, religion, political affiliation, or any number of other things).

It's tempting to think of oppression in conspiratorial terms—for example, the 1 percent plotting against the 99 percent, or men conspiring against women. But this is very often a misleading assumption. Of course, sometimes cabals do conspire to harm or exploit others, but this isn't a necessary feature of oppression. In fact, the people who benefit from oppression need not intend to oppress others and may not even be aware they are cogs in an oppressive political, social, or economic machine.

Here's an example. Most of the commercial chocolate that's consumed in first-world nations is produced in West Africa, where child slaves work on cacao farms under terrible conditions. They are beaten, abused, deprived of education, and forced into long hours of dangerous and backbreaking labor. The exploitation of child labor helps the 60-billion-dollar chocolate industry to sell chocolate inexpensively and still reap large profits. So, by consuming inexpensive chocolate, we benefit from and sustain the oppression of children. It's not just the owners of the cacao farms and the big chocolate producers who oppress African children. It's the parents who buy their kids chocolate bunnies for Easter, and those of us who dig into the aptly named "death by chocolate" for dessert.

Now, what about the concept of function? There are several different conceptions of what functions are, but the one that's most relevant to the notion of ideology is that *the function of a thing is what that thing is for*. So, the "function" of a thing could equally well be described as its "purpose," or as what it's "supposed to do." Consider washing machines. The function of washing machines is to wash laundry. We could equally well express this idea by saying that washing laundry is what they're for, or is their purpose, or is what they're supposed to do. One important spin-off of this way of understanding function is that a thing retains its function even if it can't *perform* it. A washing machine that's broken still has the function of washing laundry. In fact, it's because the machine doesn't do what it's supposed to do that we can say that it's broken or malfunctioning (or not in the right sort of environment—for example, if it's not plugged in).

Humanly crafted devices such as washing machines get their function from their designers' intentions. Their functions are what their designers designed them to do. But artifacts aren't the only kinds of things that have functions. Parts of organisms have functions too. People used to think (religious fundamentalists still think) that parts of organisms get their functions from what their designer—God—had in mind when he created them, but science gives us a better explanation. Parts of organisms have functions because evolution, not God, made them that way. Birds' wings have the function of flight because those ancestors of modern birds that were able to fly survived longer and reproduced more effectively than their wingless conspecifics, perhaps because they were better able to avoid earthbound predators. And when the winged birds reproduced, they produced chicks with wings, and they did so much better that they gradually replaced the wingless ones. This story, or one very much like it, explains why bird wings have the function that they do (and why some birds, such as kiwis, penguins, and ostriches, evolved to be flightless).[1]

In a nutshell, then, *the biological function of a thing is whatever effect that thing did that enabled individuals in past generations to reproduce more successfully than those without the thing. Because more individuals with that given thing made it on to the next generation, and then to the next, they became typical of their type of creature.* Biological functions are "backward looking" in that they're a consequence of a thing's evolutionary *history* rather than necessarily what the thing does in the present. And just like human artifacts, parts of organisms keep their functions even when they can't exercise them (a bird with a broken wing can't fly, but the wing nevertheless has the function of flight).

Ideologies acquire their oppressive function in a way that's very much like how biological items get theirs. They consist of beliefs that get reproduced and thereby spread through a population. But they aren't reproduced biologically through the replication of genes. They're reproduced culturally. And they're reproduced because they promote the oppression of some group of people while benefiting another group. Ideologies are *for* oppression—not because they are intentionally designed that way, but rather because of the history of how and why they proliferated. Something that makes ideologies especially insidious is that they are not promoted because they are *deemed* to be advantageous. We don't choose our ideologies any more than we choose our viral infections. The spread of ideologies should be seen as something akin to cognitive epidemics.

White supremacism is a clear and vivid example. White supremacism as we know it today had its roots in the transatlantic slave trade and European colonialism. It emerged and spread as a result of the rise of a capitalist economy that allowed Whites to accumulate vast wealth by exploiting the labor of Blacks and indigenous Americans, and its function was to oppress these people by justifying their enslavement and abuse. Because the circumstances of Africans and Native Americans were importantly different in key respects, I'll confine myself here to discussing the oppression of the former.

To say that slavery was big business is a vast understatement. Its scale was enormous. By the year 1820, more than 10 million enslaved Africans had survived the journey to the New World (*80 percent* of those who crossed the Atlantic to the Americas at the time were Africans). The slave-driven economy was, in the words of the historian David Brion Davis, "the world's first system of multinational production for what emerged as a mass market— a market for slave-produced sugar, tobacco, coffee, chocolate, dye-stuffs, rice, hemp, and cotton."[2] Many of Britain's opulent and stately homes were built on the backs and blood of these enslaved people laboring, and often being worked to death, in the hellish colonies of the New World. Likewise, the economic powerhouse of antebellum America depended on the labor of enslaved people. In 1861 the state of Mississippi—now the most impoverished of states—had more millionaires per square mile than anywhere else in the nation; taken together, the Confederate states had the third largest economy in the world, and were home to around 4 million enslaved human beings.

It's a mistake to think that wealthy people living in opulent homes were the sole beneficiaries of the trade in human flesh. Business boomed for merchants, shipbuilders, insurers, blacksmiths, distributors, and many others. Transatlantic slavery was a child of unfettered capitalism. Its ramifications seeped into every corner of life, and did not disappear in 1865. American slavery, and the dehumanizing attitudes that sustained it, gave rise to the brutal institutions of Jim Crow—in effect, the re-enslavement of Black Americans. This is a hideous legacy that White Americans have yet to honestly face, as is evidenced by their consistent refusal to seriously examine the issue of reparations—not just for slavery—but for the generations of oppression that Black citizens have endured.

Most of the people who benefitted from slavery weren't moral monsters. In fact, paradoxically, it was precisely because they weren't moral monsters that they performed or were complicit in morally monstrous acts. Let me dissolve the appearance of contradiction. Most of the people who benefitted from slavery were ordinary people with normal moral sensibilities who lived in an era that celebrated ideals of liberty, autonomy, and universal human rights. But their moral sensibilities created a problem for them. If Africans were human beings, enslaving them would be immorally intolerable. But if Black people weren't enslaved, the mighty economic engine that slavery fed would slow down and grind to a halt. This conflict between fellow feeling and the love of money was an ideal incubator for the belief that Black people were primitive, subhuman beings that could be exploited with impunity.

The ideology of White supremacy wasn't deliberately crafted as a strategy for oppressing Black people. Rather, the belief in Black inferiority spread among Whites because it benefitted them, and therefore became attractive and easy for them to believe. And as colonialism surged, the belief in Black inferiority—which in its most extreme forms descended to grotesque and blatant forms of dehumanization—proliferated like a virus, reproducing again and again, and spreading through the population.

Like all other ideological beliefs, dehumanization plays the political role of fostering oppression, but this is only possible because political forces mesh with our propensity for psychological essentialism and hierarchical thinking. Like all ideologies, it's a product of social contagion. Powerful social forces, interacting with equally powerful psychological ones, produce altered states of consciousness in those affected by them—states of consciousness that cause them to see other human beings, often very vulnerable ones, as less than human. Once they've taken root, we are liable to perform acts of atrocity that we would never have imagined ourselves capable of performing.

I mean this seriously. It's easy to imagine that you would be immune from such influences. You might think that, had you been a German in 1938, you would have resisted the regime, or that if you were a wealthy Southerner in 1850, you would have renounced owning slaves. You very probably believe that if you had lived as a White person in the Jim Crow South, you would never have wanted to watch a Black man being tortured, mutilated, and burned to death, or that if you had been a Rwandan Hutu in 1994, you would have never raised a machete against your Tutsi neighbors.

If you harbor thoughts like these, it's possible that they are true, but it's far more likely that they are false. It's easy to be moral heroes in our fantasies. Dehumanization isn't something that's a *choice*. Imagining that it's something that's within our conscious control is to greatly underestimate its danger. There's a lesson here that needs to be taken to heart by anyone who wants to resist dehumanization. The more confident you are of your ability to resist dehumanization, the more vulnerable you are likely to be to its uncanny power.

16 | THE POLITICS OF THE HUMAN

On June 28, 1964, just short of a year before he was brutally assassinated, Malcolm X stated, on behalf of the African American people, "We declare our right on this earth to be a human being, to be respected as a human being, to be given the rights of a human being in this society, on this earth, in this day, which we intend to bring into existence by any means necessary."

Reading these words closely and carefully, you might experience puzzlement. Rather than declaring that Black people have the right for their humanity to be recognized, he talks about the right to be a human being, and says that Black Americans intend to bring the state of being human about, along with its attendant rights and respect. These words are deeply insightful. They point to a concept of the human that's crucial for understanding how dehumanization works. Malcolm suggests—correctly, in my view—that being a member of our species isn't the same as being human, and that *Homo sapiens* can be denied humanity, robbed of it, and gain or regain it.

In this chapter I'll explore the view that, far from being an objective biological category, as most people seem to assume, the category of the human is an ideological construction that's basic to ways that human societies exercise power.

You might think that this is a fool's errand, because scientists have proved that to be human is to be a member of the species *Homo sapiens*. It's true that scientists—and anyone with a modicum of scientific education—accept that all *Homo sapiens* are human. But it's definitely not true that there's a scientific consensus that *all* humans have been, and therefore must be, members of that species. Many scientists include all members of the genus *Homo*—a group that includes extinct species such as *Homo neanderthalensis* (Neanderthals) and *Homo erectus*—under the umbrella of the human. And there are others who are even more expansive and regard earlier ancestors, such as the small, furry, ape-like creatures called *australopithecines*, as human too.

These conflicting points of view aren't really scientific disagreements, even though they're disagreements between scientists. Scientific disagreements concern *facts*. Even theoretical disputes between scientists ultimately boil down to disagreement about facts. And scientists settle these disputes by making observations to determine what the facts are. So, for the question of what it is to be human to be a scientific question, there's got to be some *possible* empirical evidence that could settle it, even if there are practical reasons why these observations can't be made.

You might think that there is some fact of the matter about which of our prehistoric ancestors were human and which ones weren't, but the evidence that would allow scientists to reach a univocal conclusion is out of reach. If only the scientists could actually examine a species like *Homo erectus*, which died out around one hundred and fifty thousand years ago, they could tell whether or not these individuals were human. Well, let's try a little thought experiment to find out. Imagine that a team of paleoanthropologists who want to answer this question have access to a time machine. They climb aboard and set the dial to 1 million years ago, so they can meet *Homo erectus* in the flesh. If this could be done, it would vastly expand our knowledge of this extinct species. The time-travelers could make observations that would answer many questions about these primates' anatomy and physiology, their social organization, and their behavior. And they could draw well-grounded conclusions about the similarities and differences between *Homo erectus* and modern *Homo sapiens*. But ask yourself whether they could make any observations to determine whether *Homo erectus* is human. What sort of evidence would answer this question? The fact is, there isn't, and couldn't be, any such evidence.

The reason why has to do with how the concept of humanness works. "Human" isn't a scientific category. It's a category from folk taxonomy. Folk taxonomies are ordinary, nonscientific systems for classifying things. Some folk-categories map seamlessly onto scientific classifications. For example, the folk category "table salt" corresponds exactly to the chemical category "sodium chloride." Because the correspondence is exact, whenever you're talking about table salt, you're also talking about sodium chloride, and vice versa. When the biologist Ernst Mayr went to New Guinea to catalog bird species, he identified 137 species and was astonished to discover that the local, preliterate people distinguished 136 of them. But the Karam, who also inhabit New Guinea, classify the large flightless cassowary as a human being—not because they are incompetent natural historians (they're not), but rather because of the peculiarities of the category "human."

Many folk categories don't have any systematic relation at all to scientific ones. Think of weeds. Very many different species of plants count as weeds, but there aren't *any* biological characteristics that they all share that sets them off from other sorts of plants. So it's literally *impossible* to map the category "weed" onto any scientific grouping. Imagine that there's an alien super-botanist from a distant galaxy who has a *complete* knowledge of the biological characteristics of Earth plants, but who has no knowledge of human ways of life. Even though there's literally nothing about Earth plants that the alien doesn't know in every detail, they wouldn't be able to tell weeds apart from other kinds of plants.

The reason why the alien would be stumped is that what makes a plant a weed is the role that it plays in certain of our social practices—practices such as gardening, farming, and lawn maintenance. Weeds are just plants that are growing where we don't want them to be growing, so the category gets its meaning from the way that humans in post-agricultural civilizations live their lives. In hunter-gatherer societies, where there is no clearing and cultivation of land, the concept of a weed would be unintelligible. Fifty thousand years ago, when everyone was a hunter-gatherer, weeds didn't exist. Weeds are an invented kind—an artifact, or social construction—even though the plants that are weeds are not. And today, in a weed-infested world, the notion is extremely elastic. What counts as a weed in one context doesn't count as one in another. A dandelion plant growing on my lawn is a weed, but if the very same plant were growing in the woods behind my house, it wouldn't be one.

I've spent so much time talking about weeds because the weed example helps us critically interrogate the concept of the human.

The relationship between the folk category "weed" and the various species of plants is very similar to the relationship between the folk category "human" and scientific categories like "Homo sapiens." The model helps, because, despite their similarities, figuring out what it means to be human is much more challenging than figuring out what it means to be a weed. It's challenging not because the question of what it means to be human is especially complicated, but rather because the notion of the human is so highly charged for us that we have a hard time thinking clearly about it.

The category of the human is a social construction. This is obvious when we look at some of the ways that it's actually been used for much of human history and across the globe. Some of the most illuminating examples come from the anthropological literature. The science of anthropology began in the nineteenth century, and from the start anthropologists noticed that there are many cultures in many different parts of the world that refer to themselves and only themselves as "the human beings" or "the real human beings." As the anthropologist Claude Levi-Strauss put it in an often-quoted passage, "Humanity is confined to the borders of the tribe, the linguistic group, or even, in some instances, to the village. . . ."[1]

The lesson to be taken from this is that when a group of people essentializes itself—sees itself as fundamentally and ineradicably distinct from all other people—the concept of the human becomes indistinguishable from the concept of "our kind." In ethnically homogeneous societies, this means members of the society are human, and everyone else is not. In heterogeneous societies where there is "racial" or ethnic diversity—that is, most modern societies—the situation is more complex. In such societies, the concept of the human is an ideological structure. It's a concept that's used to legitimate and regulate relations of domination. If, as is often the case, the dominant group essentializes itself, that becomes the paradigm of the human and all others are either lesser humans or, at the extreme, subhumans.

This view of what it means to be human has some important implications for the struggle against dehumanization. One is that it shows us that the idea of the human is a contested and unstable category. Its boundaries shift as power relations change, so invoking a common humanity to combat dehumanization is unlikely to be effective.

A second, related point is that attempts to refute dehumanizing beliefs by pointing out that we are all members of the same species is likely to fall on deaf ears. That argument could only be persuasive to someone who is already committed to the view that all *Homo sapiens* are human, and that's the very person who doesn't need to be convinced. It's quite rare in the modern world for people to deny that those whom they dehumanize are members of a different biological species (as was common in the nineteenth century and before). And there's no need for them to do so, because it is perfectly intelligible for them to hold the view that there are members of our species that aren't human.

Malcolm X understood that humanness is a political status that's brought into existence by social and political forces rather than a biological condition, and he understood that when dehumanized groups assert that they are human, it is an act of staking a claim rather than one of asserting a fact. Fighting dehumanization isn't primarily about debating facts: it's about clashing visions of what sort of world we want to live in. These are political conflicts that are deeply entwined with the psychological processes that I described earlier in this book—psychological essentialism and hierarchical thinking—that make them seem to be about facts. There's much more to be said about the underlying psychological dynamics, how these respond to political forces to produce dehumanizing attitudes, and what all this implies about resisting dehumanization. But first, we need to look at the role of political speech in the cultivation and spread of dehumanizing attitudes.

17 | DANGEROUS SPEECH

"These are the facts: a significant portion of the Gypsy population is not fit for coexistence. It is not fit for living among people. These Gypsies are animals and behave as animals."[1] These are not the words of Adolf Hitler. They are from a 2013 op-ed entitled "Who Should Not Be?" written by the outspoken journalist Zsolt Bayer, a personal friend of Hungarian prime minister Viktor Orban, and one of the thirty-seven founders of Hungary's ruling Fidesz party. He went on to list all the ways that they were depraved and like animals. He claimed that they have sex like animals, that they relieve themselves in public like animals, and that they "are incapable of any kind of communication that could be called human. Most often inarticulate sounds surge forth from their animal skulls and the only thing they understand in this miserable world is violence."

Bayer's article was ostensibly prompted by the stabbing of two Hungarian athletes in a bar fight in which Roma men were involved. Contemplating what may have moved the men to violence, Bayer moved on from using animalistic metaphors to straightforwardly laying out his view of the Roma as subhuman.

They did it because they are not people. Because they draw knives right away, even if there are forty of them, and stab. In the heart, often one time after another. Good Lord, how intolerable all this is, how it destroys everything that is human.

Bayer's tirade is a good example of what legal and human rights scholar Susan Benesch calls *dangerous speech*. Dangerous speech is any form of expression that is likely to cause others to commit or condone acts of violence against some group of people. Not all dangerous speech is dehumanizing speech. People often incite or justify violence against a group without encouraging an audience to think of their targets as nonhumans. But dehumanizing speech is an especially dangerous kind of speech, because of its power to elicit extreme forms of violence.[2]

Zsolt Bayer isn't a fringe figure. In 2016 he was awarded the Knight's Cross of the Order of Merit, one of Hungary's highest state honors. And his message is nothing new. He is just a present-day spokesman for hostility against Romani people ("Gypsies")— a tradition that dates back centuries. For the last thousand years the Romani have been expelled, enslaved, tortured, forcibly sterilized, and murdered with impunity in a series of atrocities that culminated in the Nazi genocide (known to them as *Porrajmos*, "the Devouring"), which took the lives of around 25 percent of the Romani population of Europe. Today, they are the targets of far-right violence, and suffer poverty and discrimination.

There are two factors that made Bayer's remarks especially dangerous, and which throw light on how dangerous speech works. The first is the toxic ideological background of his comments, and the second was his access to mass media, which spread his words quickly and widely.

Let's begin by looking at the background—the long, tortured history of racism against and dehumanization of Gypsies. The Romani people have been dehumanized in Europe for centuries. From the fifteenth century onward, they were described as pigs, wolves, apes, monstrous beings, and, of course, vermin. Like today's migrants and refugees, they were accused of bringing disease, and were described in language that, although centuries old, is uncannily similar to today's anti-immigrant rhetoric. The Romani were said to be "swarming," "infesting," and "plaguing" civilized society. This is classic exterminationist language, and, as the historian Miriam Eliav-Feldon points out, it fueled efforts to annihilate them. "Such verminization," she writes, "helps to explain why Gypsies were the sole target of organized manhunts from the late sixteenth century well into the eighteenth century. . . . Local authorities . . . either organized official hunts or incited the population to do so by offering rewards on Gypsy men and women, dead or alive."[3]

Although beliefs about the Romani coalesced into an ideology five centuries ago, they persist in the collective consciousness of non-Romani people, especially in Europe, to this day. Gypsies still suffer discrimination, are still regarded as filthy, disease-ridden subhumans, and are commonly assumed to be thieves and criminals in Europe. And they are still targeted with lethal violence—violence like that which erupted in the village of Hadareni, Romania, in 1993, when a Roma man stabbed one of the residents to death in an altercation. The killer and three confederates fled to their house and locked themselves inside,

fearing reprisals. Before long, townspeople, including the local po-
liceman, surrounded the house, doused it with gasoline, and set it
ablaze. Two of the Gypsy men were burned to death, and the other
two were clubbed to death by the crowd while trying to flee. The
crowd of men, women, and children could hear the dying screams
of the burning men. Twelve more Roma homes in Hadareni were
burned to the ground that day by a mob of around five hundred
Romanians and Hungarians. A reporter for the British newspaper
The Independent interviewed two of the participants in the pogrom who professed that they were "proud" of their actions:

> "On reflection, though, it would have been better if we had
> burnt more of the people, not just the houses" . . . "We did
> not commit murder—how could you call killing Gypsies
> murder?" protested Maria. "Gypsies are not really people,
> you see. They are always killing each other. They are criminals,
> sub-human, vermin. And they are certainly not wanted here."[4]

Dehumanizing ideologies can remain dormant for years,
decades, or even centuries, only to spring to life and become virulent when the political climate becomes hospitable to them. And
speech like Bayer's can be the spark that lights the volatile ideological powder keg—all the more so when the speaker has access to
mass media.

I described in chapter three that many centuries ago
dehumanizing ideas spread slowly and relatively ineffectively
through word of mouth, and how, with the advent of the printing
press and eventually widespread literacy, they proliferated much
more quickly and widely. By the twentieth century, communication

technology hugely amplified the power and reach of dangerous speech—through radio, cinema, television, and the Internet. Mass media consequently became a crucial means for promoting dehumanization. The Nazis were the first to fully grasp this point. Hitler's minister of propaganda Joseph Goebbels was quick to harness the power of the media to the Fascist cause. In 1933, the year that Hitler was appointed chancellor of Germany, he unveiled the *Volksempfänger* ("people's receiver")—an easily affordable radio that gave the masses access to entertainment, but also, crucially, propaganda. By 1941, 65 percent of German households owned a *Volksempfänger*, and it's probably no accident that persecutions of Jews were most intense in those parts of the country where radio reception was most reliable. After the demise of the Third Reich, other genocidal regimes—for example, in Cambodia, Rwanda, and Serbia—followed suit, using mass media to organize and ignite genocidal violence.

To grasp how dehumanizing speech works, it's vital to understand how propaganda interacts with ideology. If we can identify it, we have a better chance at questioning it, rather than letting it inform our own worldview. Further, we can resist it as we see it appear, putting pressure on those political leaders or media sources that help to spread it.

Genocidal violence isn't entirely caused by dehumanizing speech. Dangerous speech *ignites and organizes* the violence that's latent in preexisting ideologies. Calls on Rwandan radio to exterminate the Tutsi cockroaches wouldn't have had any effect if there hadn't been long-standing hostility against the Tutsi (who had been favored by the Belgian colonial administration) simmering away in the background. The same holds for the demonization of Bosnian Muslims in Serbian propaganda, and all the other examples. Dangerous speech doesn't conjure up atrocity out of thin air—but it can light a fire under preexisting dehumanizing beliefs and set them into lethal motion.

In this book, I've given examples of blatant dehumanization: explicit and unapologetic descriptions of others as subhuman beings. I'll give many more before the final chapter. But most dehumanizing rhetoric is not like that. It's usually subtler, and, therefore, more dangerous. The practice of explicitly describing others as less than human is nowadays often frowned upon, and is widely condemned. So, propagandists who cultivate dehumanizing attitudes most often do this indirectly. Rather than overtly referring to a group of people as animals or monsters, they describe them in ways that evoke these images in the minds of their listeners.

There are certain themes that reappear again and again in this kind of indirectly dehumanizing discourse. A common one is *criminality*. The dehumanized group is made to appear *inherently threatening*, and their criminality is represented as crudely animalistic—typically involving rape and murder. Another common theme is *parasitism*. The dehumanized group conspires to exploit the majority, sucking the blood out of decent, honest working people, and claiming privileges that they haven't earned. Images of *filth* and *disease* are also very frequent. Dehumanized groups are vectors of infection: they are *dirty* and contaminating. They are often thought of as *invaders*, outsiders who are taking us over. They're *reproducing* at an alarming rate, and they will soon outnumber us unless we do something about it. These descriptions are usually laced with dehumanizing metaphors that nudge the audience into thinking of the group as a lower order of beings. They "swarm" and "scurry" across borders to "infest" the nation. And the places where they gather are "breeding grounds" of violence and terrorism.

When a person uses language like this, they don't have to use words like "vermin" to dehumanize a group. Nudge listeners in that direction by using the right sort of evocative language and they'll connect the dots all by themselves. They'll form an image of the targets of this rhetoric as subhuman creatures, sometimes without even realizing that they are doing so, without the speaker ever having uttered an animalistic slur. And the purveyor of dehumanizing speech has plausible deniability on his side. He can say that he had no such thing in mind.

Another key component of dehumanizing speech has to do with the human tendency to generalize. Remember that dehumanization almost always starts with racialization, and when a group of people is racialized, they're seen as having a common essence. When we essentialize a group of people, we think of them as deep down all the same. The differences between individual members of the group are insignificant compared to the despicable or dangerous essence that they all have in common. This is why they're often represented as an inchoate, homogeneous mass rather than a collection of individual human beings. This obliteration of individuality is especially salient in the language used to describe migrants and refugees: they "pour" across borders in "waves" as an ominous "rising tide" that threatens to "swamp" us. Referred to in the aggregate, they do not have unique, human identities, so we can think of them as something other than human. And at the same time, this language emphasizes the large number of the beings in question, triggering our fear that they will overwhelm our countries and consume our resources.

Once a group of people is essentialized, it becomes easy to draw sweeping conclusions about all of them from a single example. This way of thinking is reasonable in domains where essentialism, or something like it, really does apply. Think of chemistry. Because chemicals really do share an essence, it's safe to conclude that what's true of one sample will be true of every sample. We can conclude from the fact that one piece of copper conducts electricity that all pieces of copper conduct electricity. These sorts of generalizations can also be successfully applied, albeit a little less reliably, in the biological realm when we generalize about species. Knowing that one diamondback rattlesnake is venomous lets you know that all diamondback rattlesnakes are venomous.

Philosophers say that such properties (electrical conductivity in the first example, venomousness in the second) are *projectable*, because we can "project" what's true of one sample to all the others, and we can draw such conclusions about unobserved cases without having to test them against evidence. You don't need to test a teaspoon of salt to know that it will dissolve in water. You just know that it will dissolve because that's the nature of salt. Suppose that someone challenged your claim that salt dissolves in water. How would you prove them wrong? You would do something like this. You would take a spoonful of salt and stir it into a glass of water. You would offer the fact that *this* spoonful of salt dissolved in this glass of water as proof of the general claim that salt dissolves in water. It would be bizarre if the other person then said, "Sure, that particular spoonful of salt dissolves in water, but what about all the other salt in the world? I don't have any reason to think that it will dissolve in water too!" This challenge would seem crazy, and one that nobody would take seriously, because when we think that things belong to natural kinds—as salt and water do—we automatically assume that their core properties are projectable.

I explained in chapter six that the idea of race is the idea that there are natural human kinds that are set apart from one another by their racial essences. People who take on board the idea of race are likely to think of racialized people in the same way that we think about rattlesnakes, copper, and salt. They're inclined to think that every member of a race has certain core properties in common, and that what's true of one member of the race is true of all the rest, because it's in their essential nature to be that way. It's because races are treated as natural kinds that a single example that confirms a racist stereotype is often taken as proof that the stereotype applies to every member of the group. So, the example of one Black rapist is taken as evidence that Black men are rapists, and one Latino gang member can be held up as confirming the claim that Latino men are criminals. The one Roma man who stabbed someone means that all Roma people are vile animals and must be persecuted.

Nobody has ever seen an example of salt failing to dissolve in water, and although there may be very rare mutant rattlesnakes that were born without the ability to produce venom, the chances of coming upon one are close to zero. But derogatory racial stereotypes are nothing like that. The idea that Romani people are essentially—and, therefore, inescapably—violent is contradicted by the vast majority of Romani people. How do racists like Bayer come to terms with this fact? How do they square the belief that violence is part of the Gypsy essence with the observation that most Gypsy people don't behave at all violently?

An essentialist mindset allows the racist to say that although few Romani people commit violent acts *all of them have it in them to do so.* Just as salt always has the propensity to dissolve, Gypsies always have the propensity to kill, and just as the bag of salt sitting in the kitchen cupboard will dissolve if placed in a bucket of water, Gypsies will kill if placed in an environment that gives them that opportunity. Gypsies who do not behave murderously have that essential murderousness locked up inside them, ready to leap out when the conditions are right.

Demagogues and propagandists exploit our vulnerability to this way of thinking by explicitly describing some members of a racialized group in dehumanizing terms, leaving it to the listeners to generalize to all the others. We saw this in Zsolt Bayer's fulminations against Gypsies described earlier in this chapter. Bayer described "a significant portion of the Gypsy population" as criminals and subhumans, without qualification. The term "a significant proportion" is vague. It could be almost all or much less than half, and its vagueness encourages an audience that is already primed with anti-Gypsy ideology to dehumanize the entire group.

President Donald Trump often makes a similar rhetorical move. At a roundtable meeting in 2018, he remarked to California lawmakers and law enforcement officials, "We have people coming into the country, or trying to come in—and we're stopping a lot of them—but we're taking people out of the country. You wouldn't believe how bad these people are. These aren't people. These are animals." These remarks caused an uproar in the national media, to which Trump's defenders replied that he was specifically referring to violent M-13 gang members rather than undocumented immigrants generally.

It's unclear from the context which of these two interpretations is the correct one, but even if we grant that Trump had M-13 gang members in mind at the time, his comments follow the same pattern as Bayer's. Apart from the fact that no members of our species are nonhuman animals, Trump refers to a portion of a racialized group, which, because of the way essentialism works, his audience is likely to extend to encompass the group as a whole. And Bayer, Trump, or any other figure who indulges in this kind of dangerous speech can clear themselves of the charge of propagating dehumanization by insisting that they were referring *only* to the violent criminal element.

18 | ILLUSION

Political leaders—especially those with an authoritarian bent— often use dehumanizing rhetoric as a means of persuasion because of its power to influence human behavior. First, they frighten us by getting us to think of some group of people as demons, monsters, or deadly predators. Then, they court our support by promising to save us from these terrors. Those who are skilled in the dark arts of political persuasion are illusionists who, under the right circumstances, can be difficult to resist. So, to resist being ensnared by dehumanizing rhetoric, it's important to understand the nature of illusion and our vulnerability to it.

Often, we think of illusions as false perceptions. Most people have had the experience of looking at a full moon hanging low on the horizon and thinking that it looks enormous. But in reality, the moon occupies exactly the same area of your visual field when it's just rising as it does when it's high in the sky, where it seems much smaller. Psychologists call this the "moon illusion." It's a perceptual illusion, but there are other illusions that have more to do with beliefs than with perceptions. A person might have illusions about themselves (for instance, they might believe that they are more intelligent, attractive, or talented than they really are) or about other people whom they know. Still other illusions are the effect of misdirection and trickery. It's not for nothing that stage magicians are also called "illusionists." The common thread uniting these three sorts of illusion is that they give us a false, distorted picture of the world.

Sigmund Freud had something to say about this. In his 1927 book *The Future of an Illusion* he presents an interesting theory of illusion. And although the book is ostensibly about religious belief (Freud thought religion a collective illusion), it is also very relevant for coming to grips with the extremely dangerous, collective illusions that dehumanizing propaganda promotes. And there is more to the analogy than this. The most dangerous political movements—the authoritarian ones that dehumanize vulnerable groups—often inspire something like religious devotion.

Unlike most writers on illusion, Freud didn't think that all illusions were false. That's because he defined illusions as *beliefs that we adopt because we want them to be true.* The moon illusion doesn't count as a Freudian illusion because it's not motivated by a desire for the moon to be large. But a person's inflated belief in their own attractiveness does count as an illusion, provided that the person who believes this believes it because they want it to be true. And on the flip side, Freud allowed that illusions don't have to be false. They can also be true. Here's an example, illustrating how this works. Consider someone who badly wants to be very attractive. And suppose that this person wants this so badly that they con themselves into believing that it's true, and they're *really* drop-dead gorgeous. They believe it because they want it to be true. But it really is true—so it's a true illusion.

Freud argued that this sort of motivated reasoning drives religious belief. Religious people (that is, most of humanity) believe in God because they are painfully and terrifyingly aware of their own helplessness in the face of the forces of nature (natural disasters, disease, and inevitable death) and the depredations of our fellow human beings. We humans are the only animals that can reflect on these harsh realities, and this awakens in us a deep longing for safety, security, and salvation, which Freud describes as "the oldest, strongest and most urgent wishes of mankind." We all want to be safe and secure. We all want to live rather than die, and we all want to be shielded from persecution and injustice.

Confronted with our vulnerability in the face of these twin threats, we're thrown back on memories of the period of life when we were at our most helpless—the experience of being small children, when we depended on our parents for our very existence. "As we already know," Freud writes, "the terrifying impression of helplessness in childhood aroused the need for protection—for protection through love—which was provided by the father and the recognition that this helplessness lasts throughout life made it necessary to cling to the existence of a father, but this time a more powerful one."[1] So religious beliefs count as illusions, even if they were to turn out to be true, because our belief in God is the result of desperate longing for salvation rather than evidence that God exists.

It's obvious that I think that Freud's story has a lot going for it. But it's also radically incomplete. Freud speaks as if the longing for a heavenly parent spontaneously emerges in the minds of human beings when they recognize the inevitable existential threats that haunt us. But nobody acquires religious beliefs that way. We're *taught* to believe in God. In the Abrahamic religions of Christianity, Judaism, and Islam (the sorts of religions that Freud had in mind), cultivating fear plays a large role in religious instruction. Without God, we are playthings of the forces of evil. We must submit to God's will in exchange for his protection. And defying his will is to court catastrophe on earth or eternal torment in the afterlife.

Religious propaganda *ramps up* ordinary feelings of helplessness and then offers an illusion of salvation from them. Like religion, politics traffics in and plays upon our deepest hopes and fears. And like religion, authoritarian political propaganda works by first making us feel endangered and then offering us a way to escape from our feelings of helplessness. In fact, political speech addresses the same two sources of helplessness that Freud identified as the wellsprings of religion. It is concerned with protections from the dangers posed by the forces of nature (for example, healthcare and the menace of global climate change) and the dangers posed by our fellow human beings (for example, crime and foreign policy). As political speech moves toward the authoritarian extremes and morphs more and more into manipulation and propaganda, the dangers posed by others become the main if not the exclusive focus, and political illusions—illusions in the Freudian sense of the word—replace rational policy solutions. And as race becomes salient in this discourse, political propaganda is on its way to becoming dangerous, dehumanizing speech.

The British psychoanalyst and philosopher Roger Money-Kyrle spelled out exactly how this works in a powerful article entitled "The Psychology of Propaganda." The article was inspired by his experience visiting Germany in 1932, the year before Hitler was appointed chancellor. Hitler campaigned frenetically that year, holding rallies all over Germany. Money-Kyrle attended some of these, and used his experiences as the basis for a compelling theory of propaganda, which he presented in this 1941 article.

Money-Kyrle's experiences in Germany got him interested in how skillful propagandists persuade audiences by manipulating their emotions—first by inducing feelings of vulnerability in them, and then offering them a way to feel invulnerable. His descriptions of the atmosphere at Hitler's rallies are very vivid. "The speeches," he wrote, "were not particularly impressive. But the crowd was unforgettable. The people seemed gradually to lose their individuality and to become fused into a not very intelligent but immensely powerful monster" that was "under the complete control of the figure on the rostrum" who "evoked or changed its passions as easily as if they had been notes of some gigantic organ."[2]

For ten minutes we heard of the sufferings of Germany . . . since the war. The monster seemed to indulge in an orgy of self-pity. Then for the next ten minutes came the most terrific fulminations against Jews and Social-democrats as the sole authors of these sufferings. Self-pity gave place to hate; and the monster seemed on the point of becoming homicidal. But the note was changed once more; and this time we heard for ten minutes about the growth of the Nazi party, and how from small beginnings it had now become an overpowering force. The monster became self-conscious of its size, and intoxicated by the belief in its own omnipotence. . . . Hitler ended . . . on a passionate appeal for all Germans to unite.[3]

Seeing how Hitler worked the crowd led Money-Kyrle to the idea that for political propaganda to work, propagandists have got to convince their audience that they need to be saved from a terrible fate. The first step is to elicit a sense of depression and humiliation—the feeling that the future is bleak, that they are a laughingstock, and so on. The next step is to drum up fear by convincing listeners that they are under threat from powerful external enemies and insidious internal ones. Finally, the propagandist offers him- or herself and the cause as the one and only path to salvation.

Money-Kyrle rightly pointed out that this technique wasn't unique to Hitler—it's used by many authoritarian political propagandists. And they don't always use it in a deliberate, calculated manner. Some of them just have a salesman's instinct for how to manipulate people.

Consider Donald Trump's speech of June 16, 2015—the speech in which he announced his bid for the Republican nomination. He begins by eliciting feelings of depression and loss. "Our country is in serious trouble," he intones. "We don't have victories anymore. We used to have victories, but we don't have them. When was the last time anybody saw us beating, let's say, China in a trade deal? They kill us. . . . They're laughing at us, at our stupidity. And now they are beating us economically." Then, having created a gloomy atmosphere, he transitions to the paranoid mode, representing good Americans as innocent victims of predatory outsiders.

When Mexico sends its people, they're not sending their best. . . . They're sending people that have lots of problems, and they're bringing those problems with us. They're bringing drugs. They're bringing crime. They're rapists. . . . It's coming from more than Mexico. It's coming from all over South and Latin America, and it's coming probably—probably—from the Middle East. But we don't know. Because we have no protection and we have no competence, we don't know what's happening.

Next, the bringer of bad news unveils his panacea. Salvation is at hand. The dangers will be banished. The problems will be solved.

Now, our country needs . . . a truly great leader, and we need a truly great leader now. We need a leader that wrote "The Art of the Deal." We need a leader that can bring back our jobs, can bring back our manufacturing, can bring back our military, can take care of our vets. Our vets have been abandoned. . . . We need somebody that can take the brand of the United States and make it great again.[4]

After repeating the first two movements a couple of times, driving his audience to a crescendo of enthusiasm (chants of "We want Trump" and "Trump, Trump, Trump, Trump, Trump"), he concludes, "Sadly, the American dream is dead. But if I get elected president I will bring it back bigger and better and stronger than ever before, and we will make America great again."

The rhetorical pattern is unmistakable. First, the speaker plays on the crowd's insecurities and grievances. He exacerbates these, conjuring up demons, and then he offers the crowd the illusion of salvation from those demons. Trump's speech stopped short of overtly dehumanizing undocumented immigrants from Mexico on this occasion. But the second stage of the process that Money-Kyrle described—the stage of inculcating paranoid terror, typically of some racialized group—often tips over into implicit or explicit dehumanization in the most toxic and dangerous forms of propaganda. The people who are painted as a threat aren't merely pictured as criminals or spongers, they are predators or disease-carrying vermin.

The leader offers his terrified audience salvation. We are all attracted to the possibility of being rescued from the frightening contingencies of life, to finding a place in the world where we and those whom we love are safe and secure. That's why the leader who promises to deliver us from evil can have such a magnetic appeal. Hitler is nowadays seen as the embodiment of hate, but the appeal of Hitler's rhetoric had little to do with hate. As historian Claudia Koonz observes:

> Hitler ... heard Germans' hunger for a government they could trust and a national purpose they could believe in. From his earliest days as a political orator he addressed that longing. . . . Hitler promised to rescue old-fashioned values of honor and dignity from the materialism, degeneracy, and cosmopolitanism of modern life. His supporters' list of grievances was long, and their anxieties ran deep.[5]

When the leader's message is leavened with dehumanizing rhetoric, his promise of salvation is all the more potent. He will banish, incarcerate, or exterminate the subhuman savages. He will cleanse the nation or the race from this infestation of filthy vermin. Drunk on the illusion, the audience feels powerful again. Depression and fear give way to manic elation—to feelings of triumph, control, and contempt—and the stage is set for an explosion of violence.

19 | GENOCIDE

"You," the soldiers said, pointing at her. She froze. "You!" She squeezed her baby tighter. In the next violent blur of moments, the soldiers clubbed Rajuma in the face, tore her screaming child out of her arms and hurled him into a fire. She was then dragged into a house and gang-raped. By the time the day was over, she was running through a field naked and covered in blood. Alone, she had lost her son, her mother, her two sisters and her younger brother, all wiped out in front of her eyes. . . ."[1]

This scene did not take place long ago in Nazi-occupied Poland, or somewhere in Rwanda during the 1994 uprising. It's from a report published in the *New York Times* in October 2017 about recent events in the South Asian nation of Myanmar. The horror experienced by Rajuma was not a singular occurrence. It was one of many stories of the suffering of the Rohingya—a Muslim minority in an overwhelmingly Buddhist nation who are victims of continuing genocidal violence.

The Rohingya live mainly in the northern part of an area known as Rakhine State, a part of the country that stretches along its western coast, and shares a border with Bangladesh to the north.

The Rohingya have lived there for more than a thousand years. The region was incorporated into Myanmar (then called Burma) when it came under British rule early in the nineteenth century.

Japan invaded in 1942, and many Burmese welcomed this as an opportunity to free themselves from the yoke of British colonialism. But the Rohingya stayed loyal to the Brits, who promised them an autonomous Muslim National Area in return (a promise that they never delivered on). This exacerbated ancient enmities and sparked violence between Rohingya and Burmese Buddhists. Hundreds of Rohingya villages were set ablaze, and as many as one hundred thousand of Rohingya were killed by their countrymen. More were raped, tortured, and killed by Japanese troops. These events led to a mass exodus of Rohingya across the porous northern border into the East Bengal (now Bangladesh). In 1982 the ruling Burmese military dictatorship government stripped the Rohingya of their citizenship, and today they are the world's largest group of stateless people, and probably the world's most persecuted.

The present-day crisis came to a head in 2012, when a Buddhist woman was murdered and allegedly gang-raped by three Rohingya men. When police announced that they had arrested three Muslim suspects, a Buddhist lynch mob assembled outside, demanding that the prisoners be released into their hands. The police refused, and a few days later ten Muslims were dragged off a bus and beaten to death. These incidents were followed by the first of several waves of anti-Rohingya violence. Villages were burned. People were hogtied and executed. Children were hacked to death with machetes. Security forces at first turned a blind eye to the brutalities, and then later participated in them.

The participation of the security forces marked a transition from mob violence to state-sponsored atrocity. More recently, attacks by Rohingya insurgents on government forces led to widespread violence against ordinary civilians. Since 2016, thousands have been killed. They've been shot, burned, or hacked to death, raped, tortured, and subjected to other human rights violations. Almost a million have fled to other countries, mainly Bangladesh, where they are detained in vast, squalid refugee camps. More than half of the refugees are children.

Dangerous propaganda has played an important role in the eruption of violence in twenty-first-century Myanmar. And although the Rohingya are the most vulnerable group, non-Rohingya Muslims are also targets. Anti-Rohingya feeling is widespread in Myanmar, but the major purveyors of racist and dehumanizing speech are militant Buddhist monks, the most prominent of whom is named Wirathu, who promulgates his poisonous message through sermons, leaflets, and, most importantly, social media.[2]

One of the striking features of the exterminationist form of dehumanization—the form of dehumanization that often leads to genocide—is how repetitive its themes are. With small, local variations, each example seems to be cut from more or less the same cloth. Almost always, the dehumanized group is regarded as an inferior race, and described as resembling predatory or unclean animals. No matter how tiny and vulnerable the persecuted population is, their dehumanizers perceive them as posing an existential threat from which they urgently need to defend themselves. Often, the dehumanizers regard those whom they dehumanize as part of a powerful, shadowy conspiracy that controls world governments and the mass media. And sex is an ever-present element. The dehumanized group is seen as hypersexual and therefore bestial. They are rapists and pedophiles, and they reproduce so rapidly that they will soon replace the dominant group as the majority.

You probably recognize some of these motifs from my descriptions in previous chapters. Let's look at how they're expressed in today's Myanmar, starting with overtly dehumanizing rhetoric.

Rohingyas are portrayed as dangerous subhuman animals or vermin. Wirathu often does this. "Islam is a dangerous and fearful poison that is severe enough to eradicate all civilization," he said. "Muslims are like the African carp. They breed quickly and they are very violent and they eat their own kind. . . . Because the Burmese people and the Buddhists are devoured every day, the national religion needs to be protected."[3] In an interview with the journalist Tin Aung Kyaw, Wirathu stated, "Snakes are poisonous wherever they are. You cannot underestimate a snake just because there is only one. It is dangerous wherever it is. Muslims are just like that."[4] "You can be full of kindness and love, but you cannot sleep next to a mad dog," he has said.[5] On other occasions he has described Muslims as "beasts, who are opposite to all in everything, and are claiming they are natives of Myanmar"[6] and proposed that "Muslims are only well behaved when they are weak. . . . When they become strong, they are like a wolf or a jackal, in large packs they hunt down other animals."[7] A 2016 op-ed in Myanmar's major state newspaper referred to the Rohingya as "detestable human fleas."[8] A 2018 investigation into anti-Rohingya hate speech on Facebook revealed that posts written in Burmese "call the Rohingya or other Muslims dogs, maggots and rapists, suggest they be fed to pigs, and urge they be shot or extermi-nated."[9] These remarks, seemingly torn from the timeless playbook on how to dehumanize the other, are not all figurative. Militant monks have seriously claimed that Rohingya are reincarnations of snakes and insects, and that killing them is equivalent to extermi-nating vermin.[10]

The Rohingya are racialized and set apart from the Buddhist majority as invaders from abroad. Even though they have lived in Myanmar for centuries, Buddhist nationalists (and govern-ment spokespersons) refer to Rohingyas as "illegal immigrants" or "Bengalis"—a term that suggests that they come from and be-long in neighboring Bangladesh. They are routinely described as "kalars"—a derogatory term for foreigners, often translated as "niggers." One posting mentioned in the Reuters report on hate speech read, "These non-human kalar dogs, the Bengalis, are killing and destroying our land, our water and our ethnic people. . . . We need to destroy their race." The author of this comment, like so many guilty of dehumanization-fueled hatred, draws a straight line from calling someone a foreigner to setting the other apart as a foreigner and less than human, scapegoating them, and calling for their death.

Muslims account for less than 5 percent of Myanmar's popula-tion, but they are nevertheless described as taking over the country and preparing for bloody jihad. For example, in a 2018 sermon posted on YouTube, Wirathu stirred up fear of the Rohingya, again calling them Bengalis to stress their otherness:

[The] Bengalis are always bloodthirsty. They have killed people of Rakhine State. They have burned Rakhine villages.

They have destroyed religion of Rakhine. When these Bengalis can come into the country without any restrictions, they are going to destroy religion of Myanmar. They are going to kill people of Myanmar. They are going to destroy the lives, shelters, and properties of people of Myanmar. . . . They are going to rape the girls of Myanmar. . . . Myanmar will soon become a land without rule of law.[11]

As is often the case for dehumanized groups, the Rohingyas are imagined to be part of a vast, evil conspiracy. Monks have claimed that the international media is biased against their cause because it is controlled by Muslims, and that nongovernmental aid organizations such as Médecins Sans Frontières supply Rohingya insurgents with weapons and explosives.[12] Writing during the Obama administration, Wirathu said that the US president is "tainted with black Muslim blood" and that "our own religion and race is more important than democracy."[13]

As in so many instances in history, sex and reproduction play an important role in this hideous discourse. Rohingya are accused of breeding so rapidly that they are on the way to replacing Buddhists as a majority, and Rohingya men are accused of being serial rapists who target Buddhist women. Wirathu made the astonishing statement in an interview for the *Asian Correspondent* that "one hundred percent of the rape cases [in Myanmar] are by Muslims"[14] and told a journalist from *The Guardian* newspaper that Buddhists are "being raped in every town, being sexually harassed in every town" by Muslims.[15] In stark contrast to these claims, the United Nations independent international fact-finding mission in Myanmar stated in its 2018 report that the Myanmar military is responsible for the brutal gang rape of hundreds of Rohingya girls and women.

> Rape, gang rape, sexual slavery, forced nudity, sexual humiliation, mutilation and sexual assault are frequently followed by the killing of victims. The scale, brutality and systematic nature of these violations indicate that rape and sexual violence are part of a deliberate strategy to intimidate, terrorize or punish a civilian population, and are used as a tactic of war. This degree of normalization is only possible in a climate of long-standing impunity.[16]

Words incite actions, and in Myanmar, this dehumanizing rhetoric has inflamed preexisting anti-Muslim bias, leading to horrendous acts of violence. The United Nations report continues, stating that the mission was "deeply disturbed by the prevalence of hate speech, offline and online, often including advocacy of national, racial or religious hatred constituting incitement to discrimination, hostility or violence":

> This has accompanied outbreaks of violence, especially in Rakhine State. Dehumanizing and stigmatizing language against the Rohingya, and Muslims in general, has for many years been a key component of the campaign to "protect race and religion," spearheaded by extremist Buddhist groups. . . . The Myanmar authorities, including the Government and the Tatmadaw, have fostered a climate in which hate speech thrives, human rights violations are legitimized, and incitement to discrimination and violence facilitated.[17]

Readers should find all of this disturbingly familiar, not only because it echoes the atrocities of the past, but also because it echoes a kind of political rhetoric that has recently been gaining ground in White nationalist and other right-wing circles in the United States and Europe, where migrants and asylum seekers are castigated as subhumans, routinely accused of being rapists, terrorists, and murderers, and are said to be supported by the so-called fake-news media.

It's hard for Americans to accept that genocidal violence is possible on their soil. The myth of American exceptionalism, and massive ignorance of the horrors of the past, make this possibility extremely difficult for many of them to confront. But as I write these words, on July 4, 2019, there are festering detention centers housing refugees who have crossed our southern border. These are places where children who have been separated from their parents sleep on concrete floors in cells and cages, and are without adequate food, water, and sanitation. They are places where parched and desperate women report that they are told to drink water from the toilets. They are places of cruelty, callousness, and despair.

When Democratic representative Alexandria Ocasio-Cortez described these as concentration camps, her remark elicited outrage and condemnation from her Republican colleagues, as well as others. But she was absolutely right to call them this. The word is unattractive, and has disturbing historical resonances, but that's because the *facts* are unattractive—punishing children for losing a comb by making them sleep on a concrete floor is unattractive[18]— and it is precisely because the historical resonances are so unsettling that we should face them, as Jewish historian and human rights scholar Anna Lind-Guzik, among others, has argued. She concluded her essay with these searing words:

> In memory of the 6 million Jews who perished because they were considered less human, I will not accept my government treating migrants like animals. And as the daughter of a Soviet Jewish refugee, I will not accept the criminalization of stateless people. Perpetrators depend on complacency, on our inability to care for people unlike ourselves. No person is illegal, or a pest to be exterminated. If you don't like the term concentration camp, help close them.[19]

To resist dehumanization, we need to be alert to its warning signs—the forms of speech that implicitly or explicitly convey the idea that some people are less than human. We must resist being desensitized to suffering, and resist blaming the victims for their plight. And we must refuse the temptation to assert that dangerous forms of speech, and the inhumane acts that follow from them, are "not the same" as those that preceded the Holocaust, or the Rwanda genocide, or the genocide of the Rohingya. They're not the same until they *are* the same, and by then it's much too late.

20 | CONTRADICTION

In the fall of 1939, Joseph Goebbels, the Reich's propaganda minister, left his usual haunts in Berlin and traveled to the city of Lodz in central Poland to visit the ghetto where thousands of Jews and Roma were confined—a place of hunger, overcrowding, degradation, and disease. Later that day, he jotted down in his diary, "Car trip through the ghetto. We get out and have a close look at everything. It's indescribable. They are no longer human beings, but animals." He continued, "It is therefore no humanitarian task, but a task for the surgeon. One has to cut here, and one must do so in the most radical manner. Or Europe will disappear one day due to the Jewish disease."[1]

Goebbels mostly talked about Jews not as animals but as members of an inferior human race. In one of his earliest publications, a pamphlet called *The Nazi-Sozi*, he wrote, "Sure, the Jew is also a human being. None of us has ever doubted that. But a flea is also an animal,—albeit an unpleasant one."[2] So we find Goebbels telling us that Jews are subhuman on one occasion, and being adamant that they are human on another. What was going on?

It wasn't just Goebbels who spoke this way. Do you remember Maria, the woman who participated in the 1993 anti-Roma pogrom in Romania? She told a reporter, "On reflection . . . it would have been better if we had burnt more of the people, not just the houses," conceding that, as much as she despised the Roma, they were people, but then she went on to insist, "We did not commit murder—how could you call killing Gypsies murder? Gypsies are not really people, you see? . . . They are criminals, sub-human, vermin." If you read Maria's words carefully, you'll notice something strange. She seems to be contradicting herself at every turn. First, she expressed regret that the mob hadn't killed more of the *people*. But right afterward she said that Gypsies *aren't really people*. Next, she said that Gypsies are criminals, but criminals are by definition *human beings*. And finally, she proclaimed that Gypsies are *subhuman* vermin. Maria seems to both assert and deny that the Roma are human beings. Whatever they are, they should be killed—of that much she is sure.

These examples are explicit, but it's even more common for people who denigrate others as animals to implicitly reveal that they recognize them as human beings. Cast your mind back to the passage from *Der Untermensch* that I quoted in chapter four. It states, "The subhuman hordes would stop at nothing in their bid to overthrow the world of light and knowledge, to bring an apocalypse to all human progress and achievement." Now, ask yourself whether it makes any sense to say that subhuman animals like rats can "bid to overthrow the world of light and knowledge." Obviously not. Only human beings can do that. So even this virulently dehumanizing anti-Semitic text implies that Jews are human beings.

What are we to make of these contradictions and inconsistencies on the part of those who dehumanize others? Some people think that they're evidence that dehumanization isn't real. They interpret them as showing that when people refer to others as vermin or animals, they're expressing contempt and disgust, or trying to humiliate and degrade them, but that they don't mean to say that these others are literally subhuman animals. These criticisms are important, and they deserve to be taken seriously. But taking them seriously doesn't mean that we've got to embrace the conclusion that dehumanization isn't real. It just moves us toward a more subtle and sophisticated understanding of the dynamics of dehumanization.

There are a couple of reasons why we should be hesitant about accepting the conclusion that dehumanization isn't real. One is that there are plenty of examples where people clearly intend their claims about sub-humanity to be taken literally. Think back to the testimony of those Rwandan killers who said that they did not recognize their victims as human, and if they had done so they couldn't have carried out the hideous acts that they did. There are other examples from other atrocities of men saying exactly the same thing. If you reject the reality of dehumanization, you have to reject this testimony. You have to claim that the genocidaires were lying, or that these were all false memories. There are also third-person reports by people like the seventeenth–century's Reverend Morgan Godwyn, who I discussed in chapter ten. Godwyn reported that his informants told him quite explicitly that Black people aren't human beings, because they lack a human soul. Instead, they are to be classed with the "brute beasts."

Finally, there are scores of scientific and theological texts written from the Middle Ages to the present—some composed by distinguished scholars and others by crackpots—that propose that certain racialized groups are subhuman (there are plenty of examples of this sentiment expressed on neo-Nazi and White supremacist websites). Whatever one might think of these people, it's hard to doubt their sincerity.

There's another reason why we should reject the conclusion. We should reject it because there's something basically wrong with the underlying argument. The argument is based on the principle that people can't believe contradictions. For example, try as you might, you can't believe both that someone is more than six feet tall and that they're less than six feet tall. Your mind just won't play ball with this. So, when people like Goebbels say that certain other people—in this case, the Jews of Lodz—are subhuman, and they also say, or at least imply, that the very same people are human beings, *it can't be that they believe both statements*. It must be that they believe one of them but not the other. But which one do they believe? It's most straightforward to suppose that when Goebbels talked about Jews as human he meant that literally, but when he called them animals he was expressing his contempt and hatred of them.

The thing is that people *can* believe a contradiction. Of course, it's logically true that a statement and its opposite can't both be true, but human psychology can't be squeezed into the rigid rules of logic. People believe in contradictions *a lot*. Sometimes it's because they don't notice that they believe two things that can't both be true. For example, a person might be opposed to abortion on the grounds that it's morally wrong to take innocent human lives, and yet support a war that's certain to result in children's deaths. Sometimes, when people see that they're committed to contradictory positions, they decide to let go of one of them. But sometimes they can't let go of either of them, because both seem to be equally true. They manage to live with the contradiction.

People can and often do have beliefs that don't add up, so couldn't this be true of Goebbels, Maria, and all the other people who dehumanize others while also acknowledging their humanity? Couldn't it be that there are people who really do believe that some members of our species are subhuman, but who can't manage to relinquish the belief that those same people are human? I think that this accurately describes what goes on in a dehumanizing mind, and that it opens the door to a much deeper understanding of dehumanization.

To resist dehumanization effectively, you've got to accept that it's real. You've got to believe that people mean the worst that they say, rather than dismissing or making excuses for it. So, be wary of claims that dehumanization is just a way of speaking and that nobody actually believes that groups of people are less than human. In the next few chapters we're going to delve much more deeply into the nature of the dehumanizing process, and you will see that it's both more complex and a great deal stranger than the picture of it that I have painted thus far.

21 | IMPURITY

There's a famous scene in *The Eternal Jew*, the notorious anti-Semitic documentary masterminded by Joseph Goebbels, that shows a river of rats swarming through sewers and cellars. The voiceover says the following:

> Where rats appear, they bring ruin by destroying mankind's goods and foodstuffs. In this way, they spread disease, plague, leprosy, typhoid fever, cholera, dysentery, and so on.... They are cunning, cowardly and cruel and are found mostly in large packs. Among the animals, they represent the rudiment of an insidious, underground destruction—just like the Jews among human beings.[1]

The aim of this footage, as well as some other parts of the film, is to elicit disgust by representing Jews not only as subhuman, but also as filthy harbingers of disease—the "Jewish disease" of Goebbels's diary entry. Nazi propagandists exploited this imagery in their propaganda posters too, portraying Jews as rats, lice, and carriers of typhus.

Themes of dirt, disease, and disgust loom large in the rhetoric of dehumanization, and not just the Nazi variety. Dehumanized populations are very often described as dirty vectors of infection, and even as disease organisms themselves. And when they're interred in concentration camps, it's not uncommon for them to be kept in unhygienic conditions and to be denied opportunities to wash, thus denying them the treatment a person would deserve while forcing them to prove the allegation that they, as a class, are unclean.

Filth and disease are repulsive, so it's in the interest of dehumanizers to instill or reinforce the belief that members of the dehumanized group are a source of pollution. But I think there's something more to this than meets the eye—something that's central to the phenomenon of dehumanization. To begin to comprehend it, we've got to turn to a deservedly famous book by the anthropologist Mary Douglas entitled *Purity and Danger: An Analysis of the Concepts of Pollution and Taboo*, first published in 1966.[2]

Douglas argues that every culture views the world through a system of categories, and that these define the natural order—a picture of the world in which everything has its allotted place, and that the idea of purity boils down to the idea of things being in their proper place within the scheme. The problem with this is that every system of categories results in anomalies—leftover things that don't fit into any of the boxes. Such things are regarded as impure and threatening.

In the last chapter, I began to build the case that when people dehumanize others, they conceive of them not simply as subhuman animals, but as both human and subhuman together. Dehumanizing propaganda often makes use of this theme. For instance, there is an anti-Semitic poster from occupied Denmark showing an immense rat. But instead of having a rat's head, it's topped with the head of a Jewish man. Even though the text on the poster reads, "Rats, destroy them," the poster doesn't depict a rat. It depicts a ratman—an impossible fusion of human being with subhuman rodent. Douglas's insights are immensely helpful for making sense of this. In the natural order of things, a human can't be a rat, and a rat can't be a human. But the poster gives us an image of an unnatural entity—one that straddles the boundaries between natural kinds. On the poster, the ratman is gazing out of its dark hole at what looks like a map of Denmark. The scene exudes an aura of menace and pollution, exactly as Douglas's theory would predict.

Because every society inevitably encounters things that violate the categories that it sanctions, every society must find ways of dealing with these anomalous things. Douglas identifies five such ways, and all of them turn out to be pertinent to the ways that dehumanized people are treated. One method is to *try to eliminate the contradiction*.[3] Dehumanizers try to strip dehumanized people of their humanity, so they're nothing but animals. For example, some slaveholders in the United Stated fed enslaved people out of animal troughs along with the plantation dogs. Another way to produce the same result is to exterminate the dehumanized group. Another method is to *physically control* the anomalous thing. Dehumanized people are beaten, raped, castrated, sterilized, incarcerated, enslaved, subjected to discriminatory laws, and denied ordinary rights and privileges.

Dehumanized people are *avoided*: they are segregated, expelled, neglected, or herded into ghettos, prisons, or concentration camps that separate them from and make them invisible to the dominant majority. Dehumanized people are *labeled*; time after time, dehumanized people are described as dangerous and dirty. They're given derogatory names and sometimes required to display certain forms of identification or distinctive forms of dress, such as the yellow star given to Jews in Germany,[4] or the blue checkered scarf that those slated for extermination were forced to wear during the Cambodian genocide.

Douglas also identifies a less obvious method—*the use of religious rituals* to restore and reaffirm the broken social order. We see this in the ritualized humiliation, punishment, and killing of dehumanized people. In a brilliant essay, the sociologist Orlando Patterson argues that spectacle lynchings were literally sacrificial rituals designed to restore the Southern social order. To many Southern Whites, a world in which Black people could claim the rights and privileges that had hitherto been reserved for Whites was a world turned upside-down—a perversion of the racial hierarchy that God and nature had intended. Spectacle lynching was reassuring to them, because it symbolically demonstrated the absolute power wielded by Whites over Blacks, and also ensured that every Black person, from childhood onward, lived in constant terror of being humiliated, tortured, and killed.

The 1893 lynching of Henry Smith is a particularly compelling example of this. Smith was a mentally disabled farmworker accused of raping and killing a four-year-old child. He was arrested in Arkansas and brought back to Paris, Texas, where his lynching had all the trappings of a sacrificial rite. An eyewitness reported the event in gruesome detail, all the while showing no sympathy for Smith:

> The Negro was placed upon a carnival float in mockery of a king upon his throne, and, followed by an immense crowd, was escorted through the city so that all might see the most inhuman monster known in human history.

This first part of the ceremony is best understood as a ritual of degradation. By presenting Smith as a king, the mob was, paradoxically, saying that he was anything but one. The ritual is reminiscent of the story, recounted in the Gospel of John, that the Romans placed a sign on the cross where the tortured Jesus hung stating, "Jesus of Nazareth, King of the Jews." It's hard to imagine that the similarity would have been lost on a crowd composed largely if not entirely of Christian churchgoers. In Smith's case, though, the mockery was not about a claim to be the Messiah. Instead, it mocked this "monster's" pretention of being a human being. Once the procession reached the designated lynching site, the physical torture began:

> His clothes were torn off piecemeal and scattered in the crowd, people catching the shreds and putting them away as mementos. The child's father, her brother, and two uncles then gathered about the Negro as he lay fastened to the torture platform and thrust hot irons into his quivering flesh. . . . Every groan from the fiend, every contortion of his body was cheered by the thickly packed crowd of 10,000 persons . . . After burning the feet and legs, the hot irons . . . were rolled

up and down Smith's stomach, back and arms. Then the eyes
were burned out and the irons were thrust down his throat.[5]

After close to an hour of this, Henry Smith was burned alive.

Dehumanization is much more complex than merely thinking
of other people as lower forms of life. When people dehumanize
others, they think of them as both human and subhuman at the
same time, and as violating the categorical distinctions that un-
derpin the natural and social order. That's why dehumanized
people are seen as harbingers of disorder, pollution, and disease.
And even though these people are almost always marginalized and
vulnerable, they're depicted and treated as though they are profoundly threatening—thus justifying the violence against them.

When we strive to resist dehumanization, we must take into
account these complexities, and understand the sense of threat
and doom that dehumanized groups evoke in those who dehumanize them. We must also take into account that once the dehumanization of some group is underway, this growing sense of
danger prompts dehumanizers to double down on their oppressive
measures, which promotes the spread of dehumanizing ideology.
Reasoning and evidence are usually impotent once dehumanization gathers momentum, so resistance needs to happen early.
Unfortunately, it's easy to ignore the warning signs, deny what's
going on, and underestimate how quickly dehumanizing beliefs
can gain traction.

22 | MONSTERS

His nickname was Nine Nine because of his habit of singling out every ninth person in a line of detainees for special treatment. "You see," said one former detainee, "he would come into the compound . . . and scream for a headcount."

> Everyone would line up in rows of five, squatted with their hands on their heads. He would then count us—one, two, three, four, five, six, seven, eight—whacking us each on the head with a club. Then he would reach number nine, and whomever that ninth person was he would beat them mercilessly. He particularly liked stomping people, and there would be blood and sometimes brains splattered everywhere.[1]

This happened in a concentration camp. It wasn't a Nazi camp or part of the Soviet *gulag*. It was a British camp in Kenya in the early 1950s set up to quell the movement known as Mau Mau. Mau Mau was the name of a rebellion among the Kikuyu, the largest ethnic group in Kenya. Its aim was to liberate Kenya from British rule, and to restore to their rightful occupants the land that these foreigners had appropriated.

When the rebellion began, panic spread through the colonial elites. And it went into overdrive after a White couple and their young son were hacked to death with machetes. Britain lost no time cracking down on the insurgency, using techniques that they had pioneered against freedom movements in India and Malaya. These included a network of concentration camps,[2] where detainees were beaten, subjected to torture (including castration and rape), made to perform hard labor, and killed.

The British had always considered the Kikuyu to be their racial inferiors. This is how they thought of all Black Africans. But once the rebellion was underway, racism coalesced into dehumanization. "Mau Mau suspects were thrown into a category all their own," the historian Caroline Elkins recounts. "Their bestiality, filth, and evil rendered them subhuman and thus without rights. . . . Detaining these subhuman creatures amounted not only to saving Africans from themselves but also to preserving Kenya for civilized white people."[3] Former colonial administrator John Nottingham confirmed that when a rebel was shot, "All they were shooting was a wild animal. Not a human being. Or if they were beating . . . a wild animal, then they were just beating a wild animal, and not a human being."[4] Accused of cannibalism, sexual depravity, and bloodthirsty savagery, the Mau Mau rebels were no longer mere subhuman animals. They were monsters, hell-bent on exterminating the Whites. No treatment was deemed too harsh for these devils in human form—not even the brutality handed out by men like Nine Nine.

The Mau Mau insurgents were just one recent instance of a long line of humans made into monsters. When people seek to dehumanize a person or a group, they commonly describe the object of their fear, hatred, and disgust as monsters (or demons, devils, or fiends, which amount to the same thing), either explicitly or implicitly. During the Middle Ages, Jews were represented as demonic beings who consorted with the Devil. They had horns and tails. They kidnapped and cannibalized Christian children, and conspired to destroy Christian civilization by poisoning the water with bubonic plague. During the Crusades, Christians depicted Muslims as monstrous beings. One medieval chronicler described the Saracens as "a fiendish race . . . deformed by nature and unlike other living beings, black in color, of enormous stature and inhuman savageness,"[5] a description that could just as well have been an excerpt from a racist tract from the Jim Crow era, when the African American male was described as "the most horrible creature upon the earth, the most brutal and merciless . . . a monstrous beast, crazed with lust. His ferocity is almost demoniacal."[6] As we've seen, lynching victims were often described in the media of the day as monsters and fiends. And you'll recall I pointed out in chapter four that image of Jews in *Der Untermensch* makes them sound like something out of a horror film. I could give many more examples.

So how does it happen that, through dehumanization, people come to think of others as monsters? To understand how this happens, we first need to form a clear idea of what monsters are. In his wonderful book *The Philosophy of Horror*, philosopher Noël Carroll turns to works of horror fiction to figure out what properties all monsters have in common. He identifies two of them: *physical threat* and *cognitive threat*. I prefer the term *metaphysical threat* for the second of these, because I think it better captures the underlying idea.

The meaning of the notion of physical threat is evident. Monsters are malevolent. They're out to get you. They want to kill you, take you over, suck your blood, devour your flesh, and so forth. That monsters are physically threatening is reason enough to be terrified of them. But it's not enough to *make* them monsters, because physical threat alone doesn't distinguish monsters from other dangerous beings. Serial killers and grizzly bears are physically threatening, but they're not monsters.

Monsters have also got to be *metaphysically threatening.* "Metaphysics" is a term that philosophers use for the study of the fundamental structure of reality. It's concerned with what kinds of things exist and the relationship between those kinds. Something poses a metaphysical threat if it undermines your conception of the basic structure of reality. If everything that exists is in some sense "natural," then metaphysically threatening things are disturbingly *unnatural.* They are lesions in the orderly cosmos.

The best illustration of metaphysical threat that I know of is a passage from Arthur Machen's novel *The House of Souls.* "What would your feelings be," a character asks, "... if your cat or your dog began to talk to you, and to dispute with you in human accents?" He goes on:

You would be overwhelmed with horror. I am sure of it. And if the roses in your garden sang a weird song, you would go mad. And suppose the stones in the road began to swell and

grow before your eyes, and if the pebble that you noticed at
night had shot out stony blossoms in the morning?[7]

It's easy to see why physical threats are terrifying. Being cornered
by a rabid dog is terrifying because the dog might harm or kill
you. But what's so scary about a talking dog? Or singing roses? Or
blossoming pebbles? None of these things can hurt or kill you, but
they're nevertheless the stuff of nightmares. How come?

Another way to understand that special terror that's elicited
by metaphysically threatening things comes from logic, oddly
enough. Logicians hate contradictions, because anything follows
from a contradiction. In logic, this is a weird technical point about
the conditions that make if/then statements true. But the principle that anything follows from a contradiction also has existential significance that reaches far beyond the dry technicalities of
formal logic. Think of it this way: If roses can sing or dogs can
talk then *anything* can happen. The world becomes unpredictable
and dangerous. What seemed like firm epistemic ground crumbles
away beneath our feet.

A singing rose is disturbing, but it isn't a monster because it isn't
physically threatening. The rose plant would become a monster if
it reached out thorny tendrils to strangle a passerby. Zombies are
monsters because they're both alive and dead, which makes them
metaphysically threatening, and they gorge on people's brains,
which makes them physically threatening. Werewolves are simul-
taneously wolves and humans, and they tear you apart with their
fangs. The malevolent doll Chucky from the movie *Child's Play* is
an inanimate doll and an animate human, and he's also a remorse-
less killer. Dehumanized people are monsters because they're both

human and subhuman, and they're also criminals, or terrorists, or enemies of the people.

If you doubt that anyone could truly conceive of others as completely human and also completely subhuman, take a moment to contemplate how easily this way of thinking comes to you. If you've ever enjoyed a horror film—say, one about the living dead—you had no difficulty thinking of the zombies as both living and dead. You didn't think of the zombies as partially living and partially dead (for example, as having living arms and dead legs). That wouldn't be horror, because it wouldn't be contradictory. Instead, you thought of them as fully alive and fully dead. And if you've ever been terrified by the horror classic *The Exorcist*, you effortlessly accepted that a single body can be home to a twelve-year-old girl and an ancient Babylonian demon.

But in the realm of real life, not horror movies, how do our minds manage to think that a single entity can be at the same time human and subhuman? Imagine watching a stage magician perform their act. Such people can do strange things. They can present some object—say, a bouquet of red roses—and make it seem to vanish right before your eyes. The performance is captivating because it presents you with a puzzle. You know that the roses haven't simply vanished, because you know that bouquets don't just disappear. And yet, you can't help seeing them as having disappeared. Your mind tells you one thing, but your eyes tell you another.

Magicians seduce us into *almost* believing that the impossible has happened. It's "almost" believing because we know that the magician is somehow pulling the wool over our eyes, even though we don't know how he does it. We know the roses haven't really disappeared, that the ball isn't really floating in the air above the stage, and that the magician's assistant hasn't really been sawn in half.

Now imagine a situation where this happens. A guest comes to your home with a bottle of wine in her hand. She places the bottle on the dining room table right in front of you, snaps her fingers twice, and the bottle vanishes. This wouldn't be entertaining. It would be unsettling. Witnessing it, you might wonder if you are dreaming, or if you're going mad. The disappearing bottle would undermine your sense of reality in a very fundamental way. You'd be burdened with a pair of incompatible beliefs: one, based on your eyes, tells you that the wine has disappeared—and the other, based on what your mind tells you, that bottles of wine can't vanish into thin air. And you can't abandon either of them.

Often, the evidence of our senses is evidence enough. You believe that something's salty because it tastes salty, that something's purple because it looks purple, that something's hot because it feels hot. But there are other beliefs that don't depend on our direct experiences. You probably believe that everything is made of atoms, that the moon orbits Earth, and that George Washington was the first American president. But you've never *seen* these things. You've accepted them because of what others have told you—in person, in books, or from other sources. It's beliefs like these that make cumulative knowledge and culture possible. But this form of belief also introduces a vulnerability into our mental lives—one that gets exploited by propagandists who get us to accept dangerous ideas in defiance of what our senses tell us.

The two kinds of beliefs have different psychological properties. Those that are based on our immediate experiences are very forceful and vivacious. They're very hard to shake. You can look at an optical illusion and know that it's an illusion without this making any difference to your experience of it. The other beliefs, the more "cognitive" or theoretical ones, can also be hard to revise, but for a different reason. It's hard to let go of them if they're promoted by people who are supposed to know, or if they play into our prejudices, or if we think there's a high cost attached to being mistaken.

To see how the two varieties of belief contribute to dehumanizing states of mind, think about how we identify things. We usually do this based on how they appear to us. Presented with a white metal ring, you might judge it to be made of silver because you've seen lots of silver jewelry, and they all looked just like this ring. But suppose you take the ring to a jeweler, and the jeweler tells you that it's made of platinum. Even though you've never seen a platinum ring before, you outsource your judgment to the jeweler's authority and trade in your old belief about the ring for the new one. That's exactly what you should do, because the jeweler really does know things about precious metals that you don't have access to.

Now, let's compare this to what goes on in cases of dehumanization. When we encounter another member of our species, we *automatically* see them as human. But we form dehumanizing beliefs in an entirely different way. Dehumanizing beliefs are theoretical rather than perceptual beliefs. We get them from outside of ourselves—from propaganda and ideology, and from the testimony of those who are supposed to be authorities.

When we accept the view that some group of people are less than human, we have to overrule the evidence of our senses. At this point, a problem arises, because even though a person has accepted that these others aren't human, they can't stop themself from recognizing the other's humanity. So instead of exchanging the belief that the people in this group are human for the belief that they're not, the dehumanizer ends up with two contradictory beliefs. The belief that these people are human coexists in your brain with the belief that they're subhuman. Now add some physical threat to the mix. Those who dehumanize have been told, and have come to believe, that these others are dangerous—that they're murderers, rapists, drug dealers, or gang members, and that they might even pose an existential threat to their people. When all these elements are in place, a human group has been transformed into a mass of monsters.

23 | CRIMINALS

In our increasingly secular world, the idea that dehumanized people are literally demonic or in league with Satan has lost credibility, except in religious fundamentalist circles. This did not eliminate the idea that dehumanized people are monstrous or demonic—it simply cast the basic idea in a different mold. The medieval idea of essentially demonic people gradually morphed, from the seventeenth century onward, into the idea that there are essentially criminal ones.

The lynching epidemic of the late nineteenth and early twentieth century, and the mass incarceration of Black Americans that came in its wake, was driven by the idea that Black people—especially Black men—are criminal to their core. This was the received wisdom among many Whites, both in the North and in the South. Hinton Rowan Helper, whom Lincoln appointed as US consul in Argentina, wrote graphically of the "crime-stained blackness of the negro," which he fleshed out in a popular White supremacist diatribe:

In every district and community of considerable size, on the right hand and on the left, they are almost constantly committing brutal murder and highway robbery; breaking into dwellings and warehouses; depredating on orchards, fields of grain, and granaries; appropriated to their own use other people's cattle, pigs, and poultry; stealing everything that they can lay their hands upon; outraging pure and innocent white girls; and not infrequently, in a spirit of the most savage wantonness and revenge, setting on fire and utterly destroying the houses of their white neighbors. Terrorism reigns supreme among the white females of every family, and sleep is banished.[1]

The picture of Black men as predatory animals was promoted by White women as well. The image of the Black male, and the vicious attitude that accompanied it, was succinctly expressed by the suffragette (and later senator) Rebecca Felton, who declared "if it takes lynching to protect women's dearest possession from drunken, ravening beasts, then I say, lynch a thousand a week if it becomes necessary."[2] This picture of Black men has never fully dissipated. During the 1990s, political scientist John Delulio popularized the term *superpredator* for a new edition of the racial monster trope. He described superpredators as vicious, degenerate young men who gather in "wolf packs" to hunt down, rape, and murder innocent victims. When five Black teenagers—christened the Central Park Five—were falsely accused of brutally raping a New York jogger, future president Donald J. Trump spent eighty-five thousand dollars on four full-page newspaper ads calling for their death, writing, "I want to hate these murderers and I always will. I am not looking to psychoanalyze or understand them, I am looking to punish them. . . . I no longer want to understand their anger. I want them to understand our anger. I want them to be afraid."[3] Not to be outdone, conservative pundit Patrick Buchanan urged, "If the eldest of that wolf pack were tried, convicted and hanged in Central Park . . . and the thirteen- and fourteen-year-olds were stripped, horsewhipped, and sent to prison, the park might soon be safe again for women."[4]

Even though the Central Park Five were eventually exonerated on DNA evidence, after serving time in prison for a crime they did not commit, Trump continues to claim that they are guilty.[5] In doing so, he conforms to the dehumanizing logic of racial essentialism. If Black males possess a superpredatory essence, then they are fungible. *They are guilty of rape and murder even if they never commit rape or murder, because they have rape and murder in them.* As Yusef Salaam, one of the five, put the point, "We were convicted because of the color of our skin."[6]

More recently, dehumanized people of color have again been in the news. If President Trump and his cohort are to be believed, vicious Brown monsters have been swarming across our southern border from Mexico and Central America. He proclaimed at a 2017 rally in Youngstown, Ohio, that "these animals . . . take a young, beautiful girl, 16, 15, and others and they slice them and dice them with a knife because they want them to go through excruciating pain before they die. And these are the animals that we've been protecting for so long."[7]

Dehumanized people aren't always imagined as superpredators, partly because this is a gendered category that's mainly reserved for males, and partly because there are forms of dehumanization that don't involve the crucial element of physical dangerousness (I discuss this in chapter twenty-five). However, the image of the predatory monster is an important component in a great deal of dehumanizing propaganda, and it can strike a deep chord in us, because it triggers some of our most primal fears. Superpredators aren't just criminals, and they aren't even just violent criminals. They are subhumans endowed with superhuman powers.

This idea is commonly found in dehumanizing belief systems. Dehumanized people are formidable, monstrous, demonic. I've already discussed the anti-Semitic idea that Jews control the entire world—a theme frequently represented in Nazi and neo-Nazi propaganda as an enormous octopus emblazoned with the Star of David, whose tentacles envelope the world, and in the famous *Protocols of the Elders of Zion*, which purports to be a record of the Jewish project of world domination. We find a variation on the same basic theme in White people's images of Black men from the post–Civil War period onward. Whereas Jewish men were supposed to be endowed with superhuman, demonic intelligence, Black men were supposed to possess superhuman physical powers—an aspect of dehumanization that psychologists Adam Waytz, Kelly Marie Hoffman, and Sophie Trawalter call "superhumanization."[8] Not long before their paper on superhumanization was published, Waytz, Hoffman, and Trawalter wrote an article for the *Washington Post* arguing that police officer Darren Wilson's description of his encounter with Michael Brown, whom he fatally shot in Ferguson, Missouri, in the summer of 2014, suggested that Wilson superhumanized Brown. Wilson told the grand jury that investigated the shooting the following:

The only way I can describe it, it looks like a demon, how angry he looked. . . . He turns, and when he looked at me, he made like a grunting, like aggravated sound and he starts, he turns and he's coming back towards me. . . . At this point it looked like he was almost bulking up to run through the shots, like it was making him mad that I'm shooting at him. And the face that he had was looking straight through me, like I wasn't even there, I wasn't even anything in his way.

The psychologists plausibly commented, "Although unclear whether Wilson's 'it' refers to Brown's facial expression, or Brown himself, the use of the term, 'demon,' both sub-humanizes and super-humanizes Brown, clearly casting him outside of humanity."[9]

The idea of inherent criminality is at the core of the superpredator myth. In the present-day United States, Black and Latino males are most often tarred with this brush. However, the idea of the racialized criminal is quite widespread—both historically and culturally. Romani people have been regarded as essentially criminal for centuries, and this was (and is) used as a pretext for persecuting them. And the claim that criminality is part of the Jewish essence was a mainstay of Nazi propaganda used to justify their mass incarceration, over-aggressive policing, and ultimate extermination. Michael Berkowitz examines this in great detail in his book *The Crime of My Very Existence: Nazism and the Myth of Jewish Criminality*:

National Socialism actively cultivated the association of Jews with criminality.

Jews needed to be contained and closely watched, the Nazis contended, because of their propensity to criminality, and they had to be dealt with aggressively, because Jewish communal existence was an incubator for vice. A great amount of thought, energy, and effort was directed, then, to substantiating the stereotype that Jews . . . were always and preeminently a community of crooks, and that the key to managing and controlling Jews en masse was to deal with the phenomenon of Jewish criminality.[10]

Jews were incessantly represented as rapists, pimps, drug dealers, thieves, and swindlers. The notion that Jews are essentially predatory is explicit in a memo from the Nazi Periodical Service stating, "It is expected that German periodicals will . . . conduct the orientation on Jewish guilt with a tenacity that leaves no doubt in the mind of anyone that every single Jew, wherever he is and whatever he does, is an accessory to crime."[11]

It's possible to describe someone as a monster without ever using the word *monster*. Unlike the dehumanizing rhetoric of centuries past, present-day dehumanizing rhetoric uses words like "demon" and "monster" figuratively, if at all. Today, the figure of the racialized criminal is the embodiment of monstrousness in developed nations. To resist dehumanization, it is vital to resist the idea that any group of people are inherently, irredeemably criminal. This kind of rhetoric is a danger signal that the members of this group are, or will soon be, considered as less than human.

24 | CRUELTY

The philosopher Kwame Anthony Appiah once commented that the claim that genocidal killers think of their victims as subhuman animals is "not quite right," because "it doesn't explain the immense cruelty—the abominable cruelty, I'm tempted to say—that are their characteristic feature." He continued:

> The persecutors may liken the objects of their enmity to cockroaches or germs, but they acknowledge their victims' humanity in the very act of humiliating, stigmatizing, reviling, and torturing them. Such treatments—and the voluble justifications the persecutors invariably offer for such treatment—is reserved for creatures we recognize to have intentions, and desires, and projects.[1]

The virulent anti-Black racism that swept through the South in the aftermath of the American Civil War and the epidemic of lynching that followed in its wake illustrate Appiah's insight all too well. Before emancipation, White people typically regarded Blacks as "docile but irresponsible, loyal but lazy, humble but chronically given to lying and stealing; his behavior full of infantile silliness and his talk inflated with childish exaggeration. His relationship with his master was one of utter dependence."[2] And when Black people were dehumanized, they were more often seen as livestock than as monsters. But this soon changed. The image of the monstrous, rapacious, murderous Negro became a mainstay in popular culture and the media—including the blockbuster film *The Birth of a Nation*, which was screened in the White House in 1915, and apparently endorsed by President Woodrow Wilson. *The Birth of a Nation* was a movie adaptation of Thomas Dixon Jr.'s novel *The Clansman*, which presented the Ku Klux Klan as restoring order to the chaotic, war-ravaged South by putting Negros back in their proper place. Of course, the cast of characters included a Black rapist, who is lynched by the Ku Klux Klan. Less than a year later, the movie inspired the rebirth of the Klan, which had fizzled out around forty years before, and it inspired many thousands of Americans to support the White supremacist cause.

One year later, in the spring of 1916, a fifteen-thousand-strong mob lynched a teenage boy named Jesse Washington in the city of Waco, Texas. He was convicted of raping and murdering a fifty-three-year-old White woman in the nearby hamlet of Robinson. The all-White jury deliberated for all of four minutes before pronouncing him guilty. Immediately, a man stood up in the back of the courtroom and bellowed, "Get the nigger!" A lynch mob seized the young man, dragged him out of the courthouse, ripped off his clothes, wrapped a long chain around his neck, and made him walk to the town square, pushing, prodding, stomping, and stabbing him until he was covered in blood. Once they reached their destination, the mob amputated Jesse's toes, fingers, ears, and penis. They rubbed coal oil all over his bleeding body, flung the chain over a tree limb, and hoisted him up over a bonfire. They then lowered Jesse into the fire and raised him up again repeatedly, taking every step possible to prolong his agony. Two hours later, as souvenir hunters were picking through his smoldering remains, a man rode up on horseback, flung a lasso around the charred torso, and dragged it through the town. When the head came off, children pulled out the teeth and sold them as souvenirs. Then, what was left of the blackened remains of this young man's body was tied behind a car and dragged to the town of Robinson, stuffed into a burlap sack, and hung from a telephone pole.

Appiah was right when he wrote that the abominable cruelty has something to do with the fact that dehumanizers see their victims as human beings. It is because dehumanizers cannot help recognizing that their victims are human, and this recognition coexists in their minds with the belief that they are animals, that the members of the dehumanized group are regarded as horrific monsters, and such monsters are, by definition, malevolent, evil beings. And because those who are dehumanized come to be seen as evil, they become targets of the most extreme forms of moralistic aggression. The magnitude of their wickedness is such that no imaginable punishment is too severe for them.

In addition to the barely imaginable physical cruelty handed out to people like Jesse Washington, there is another element that begs for an explanation. Almost always, dehumanizers take pains to humiliate those whom they dehumanize. It is not enough to mutilate, burn, or gas the victim. The dehumanized person must be made to feel that they are lowly creatures, undeserving of consideration and respect. An explanation for this behavior is not difficult to find. Recall that dehumanization begins as a way of diminishing others—to think of them as *mere* animals. But because dehumanizers are unable to stop seeing their victims as humans, the victims are inadvertently transformed into monsters. Monsters are far removed from mere vermin: they are uncanny and endowed with superhuman powers. They are profoundly threatening and dangerous. Because of this, dehumanizers feel compelled to diminish their own creations—to render them mere animals again. Like many Black people, Jesse Washington was a monster in the eyes of his persecutors. The ritual of lynching was a way to degrade him, to strip him of his monstrousness by obliterating his humanity and rendering him entirely subhuman—an animal to be skinned, castrated, and burned on the barbecue.

There are many different ways to be human, but relatively few ways of being a human monster. The examples of demonizing dehumanization all involve variations on a few basic themes. Recall that Nazi ideology pictured Jews as the supremely powerful, demonic enemy of the German people, who combatted them with guile and superhuman intelligence rather than brute force. In 1938, Austrian Jews were literally brought to their knees to scrub the pavements of Vienna before being exported to slave labor camps or to die in the Polish extermination factories. "This was a ritual humiliation," writes historian Timothy Snyder. "Jews . . . were suddenly on their knees performing menial labor in front of jeering crowds. . . . A journalist described 'the fluffy Viennese blonds, fighting one another to get closer to the elevating spectacle of the ashen-faced Jewish surgeon on hands and knees before a half dozen young hooligans with swastika armlets and dog-whips.'"[3] The Indians of North America were also explicitly characterized as savages, devils, demons, and monsters that reveled in the blood of White settlers. They were to be starved and abused in concentration camps called "reservations," and ultimately exterminated. The well-known literary figure William Dean Howells wrote in an essay celebrating the centennial of the United States that mere contact with these creatures provides justification enough for degrading them.

> The red man . . . is a hideous demon, whose malign traits can hardly inspire any emotion softer than abhorrence. In blaming our Indian agents for malfeasance in office, perhaps we do not sufficiently account for the demoralizing influence of merely beholding those false and pitiless savage faces; moldy flour and corrupt beef must seem altogether too good for them.[4]

The language of demonization, whether subtle or explicit, is always dangerous. Whenever those in power represent members of a racialized group as monsters in human form, the stage is set for human rights abuses or worse. When people in positions of power and influence speak of others as monsters, or indulge in such rhetoric, it's a sign that a particularly destructive form of dehumanization is in the offing.

25 | DEHUMANIZATION AND ITS NEIGHBORS

We're getting close to the end now. At this point, you understand my views on what dehumanization is and how it works, and you understand my position on the close relationship between dehumanization and racism. But I've not explained the relationship between other, nearby, destructive social beliefs and practices—things like sexism, ableism, and transphobia. Often, people lump all of these together under the heading of dehumanization, but in my opinion that's a big mistake. Sexism works differently than racism, which works differently from ableism, and so on. They each have their own unique dynamics, and blurring the distinctions between them only makes it more difficult to resist them.

I've studied racism for a long time, but I'm far from having expert knowledge of sexism, ableism, and transphobia (not to mention all the other "-isms" that I haven't named). That being said, I think that the theoretical apparatus I've developed over the years is helpful both for distinguishing dehumanization from these other phenomena, and distinguishing these phenomena from each other.

Also, I hinted earlier on that there's more than one kind of de-humanization. Not all dehumanization is of the sort that makes monsters. It's not always the case that dehumanized people are seen as dangerous, cruel, and malevolent, with greater-than-human powers. I call this *demonizing dehumanization*, and it's the kind of dehumanization that I've mainly focused on in this book. But there's also *enfeebling dehumanization*.

I've explained that in my view dehumanized people are seen as both human and subhuman. Sometimes, both sides of this binary are salient, and the dehumanizer can't but see their victim as a monster. At other times, one or the other of these is in the foreground of awareness, with its counterpart in the background. When this happens, either the person's subhumanity is most salient or their humanity is. I am reminded of the testimony of a Japanese veteran who committed atrocities in China during World War II, including rape and wanton murder. He told an interviewer that when Japanese soldiers raped Chinese women they thought of them as women, but when they killed them they thought of them as pigs. But no matter which of these configurations dehumanization takes, the dehumanized person is represented in the dehumanizer's mind as both human and subhuman.

What makes the difference between demonizing dehumanization and enfeebling dehumanization is the presence or absence of physical threat. When people are demonized, they're seen as both physically threatening and metaphysically threatening. And their metaphysical dangerousness amplifies their physical dangerousness (a werewolf is more dangerous than a wolf, and a vampire that's morphed into a bat is more dangerous than a normal bat). This turns them into monsters. In contrast, when people get dehumanized in the enfeebling mode, they're seen as metaphysically threatening but physically innocuous. They may be human sheep, but they're not monsters.

Today, enfeebling dehumanization is probably less common than it was in the past, and it is probably less common than demonizing dehumanization. There are circumstances, however, that often promote it. One such is military combat, when enemy soldiers (or civilians) are pictured as prey and war as a hunting expedition. This happened in the Vietnam War, when American soldiers went "gook hunting"—that is, going off to kill Vietnamese people for fun.

The monkey is a common enfeebling representation. Traditionally, apes and monkeys were seen as incomplete or defective human beings, or as creatures occupying an intermediate position between animals and humans that could imitate or "ape" humans. European colonists accordingly thought of the people whom they oppressed as ape-like subhumans—mere simulacra of true human beings. The Irish, who were at one time considered a separate race by both their British colonizers and many Americans, were often portrayed as ridiculous apes, as were Black people in the British colonies and in the antebellum United States (the representation of Black people as apes persisted long after the Civil War, but it morphed into the image of the Black man as a predatory ape).

Enfeebling dehumanization is also associated with slavery, because slaveholders have often conceived of enslaved people as livestock or pets. Although not typically regarded as physically weak, enslaved people were often thought of as docile and dependent on their masters. Gender is relevant to the demonizing/enfeebling dichotomy, as well. It's usually men that are dehumanized as monsters, while women are dehumanized as pets or as farm animals fit for breeding. Enfeebling dehumanization is also a factor when unarmed civilians get attacked by military or paramilitary forces. This was evident in the Darfur genocide of the nearly two thousand. Villagers reported that the attackers shouted out things like, "They called her . . . dog, son of dogs," and, "We came to kill you and your kids"; "You donkey, you slave; we must get rid of you"; "You blacks are not human. We can do anything we want to you. You cannot live here"; "We kill our cows when they have black calves—we will kill you too"; and "You blacks are like monkeys. You are not human."[1]

Dehumanization is often confused with other types of derogatory attitudes. As we have seen, there is a very close relationship between racism and dehumanization. Indeed, you can't properly understand dehumanization without properly understanding race. But that tight relationship between racism and dehumanization doesn't apply to the relationship between dehumanization and sexism, ableism, and transphobia, for reasons we can understand by using the theoretical apparatus that helps us understand dehumanization. Let's start with sexism.

There are several texts in feminist theory that talk about what the authors call the "dehumanization" of women. In that literature, dehumanization is often equated with objectification—roughly, conceiving of women as things rather than as subjects and agents. One of the most powerful pieces of writing on the dehumanization of women is Catharine MacKinnon's searing essay "Are Women Human?":

If women were human would we be a cash crop shipped from Thailand in containers into New York's brothels? Would we be sexual and reproductive slaves? Would we be bred, worked without pay our whole lives, burned when our dowry money wasn't enough or when men tired of us, starved as widows when our husbands died (if we survived his funeral pyre), sold for sex because we are not valued for anything else? Would we be sold into marriage to priests to atone for our family's sins or to improve our family's earthly prospects? Would we, when allowed to work for pay, be made to work at the most menial jobs and exploited at barely starvation level? Would our genitals be sliced out to "cleanse" us (our body parts are dirt?), to control us, to mark us and define our cultures? Would we be trafficked as things for sexual use and entertainment worldwide in whatever form current technology makes possible? Would we be kept from learning to read and write?[2]

MacKinnon's catalog of abuses and degradations is horrific, but it doesn't suggest that women are dehumanized in the sense that I mean when I talk about dehumanization. On my account, women aren't dehumanized *as such*. In other words, when women are dehumanized, it's not because they're women. It's because of how they're racialized.

Let me explain why I see it this way. When people racialize another group of people, they have to do two things. First, they've got to attribute a racial essence to every member of the group— one that's not shared by any other group. And second, this essence has to be seen as transmitted by descent, and when that group of people is dehumanized, their imagined racial essence becomes an imagined subhuman essence that's transmitted by descent from one generation to the next. The logic of dehumanization is such that if your parents are subhuman, then you're subhuman too.

Sexism can't work that way because gender isn't normally understood as being transmitted by descent. Like races, genders are considered to be natural kinds in our ordinary folk taxonomies. And because they're natural kinds, they're supposed to have essences. But it can't be that gender essences are imagined to be transmitted down the bloodline by descent, like racial essences are. In other words, nobody thinks that a person is female because her parents were female. This feature sets gender apart from race and sub-humanity. How then should the sexist mindset be understood? I don't know, but my best guess is that sexists conceive of women as having a malformed human essence. Being female is seen as a chronic, unrectifiable disability. Of course, women can be dehumanized as well, but they are not dehumanized *because* they are women. When they are dehumanized it's because they belong to a racialized group that's conceived by others as less than human.

This brings us to the topic of ableism: the derogation of people with disabilities *because* of their disability. Derogatory attitudes toward people with disabilities are extremely varied—in part because disabilities are extremely varied—and a good analysis of ableism needs to be correspondingly complex. Addressing this topic in the detail that it deserves would require a book all its own. There are some general characteristics, however, that distinguish ableism from dehumanization on one hand, and from racism, sexism, and transphobia on the other.

Unlike the case with gender, it's in principle possible for disabled people to be dehumanized *as such*, although this is probably quite rare if it occurs at all. This is possible because, unlike gender, some disabilities can be transmitted by descent (or are believed to be transmitted by descent). However, it is more common for ableism to be a mirror image of dehumanization. Dehumanized people are seen as human on the outside but subhuman on the inside. But in some cases of disability, this relation is flipped. If the external appearance of the disabled person departs significantly from what is regarded as normal, others don't automatically respond to them as human beings, despite being aware that they are human. The upshot is that disabled people are often experienced as metaphysically threatening. They are regarded as impure, unnatural, and as violations of the natural order—objects of defensive mockery, horrified fascination, and, all too often, discrimination, exploitation, and violence.

Finally, transphobia: In the prevalent folk theory of gender, each of us has a gender essence that, because it is an essence, is unalterable. And contrary to the distinction between gender (a social category) and sex (a biological category), it is a prevalent folk theoretical assumption that a person's gender is a manifestation of their sex. As a result, in our culture, many people insist that it's impossible for a person to change their gender. Once male, always a man. Once female, always a woman.

Because gender essences aren't thought of as being transmitted by descent, this means that transgender people can't be dehumanized in my sense of the word. But they can be (and are) nevertheless experienced as metaphysically threatening. Consider a transgender woman—a person who identifies as a woman, but was assigned the sex "male" at birth and raised as a boy. Now, let's consider two scenarios. In one, the transgender woman has recognizably masculine characteristics as well as recognizably feminine ones, and these elicit mixed responses in others. They respond to her both as a man and as a woman. She's experienced as straddling two distinct natural kinds, and is therefore felt to be metaphysically threatening. In the second scenario, the transgender woman does not have observably masculine characteristics. In this case too, though, she may be experienced as metaphysically threatening by people who know (but don't see) that she is transgender.

Transphobic attitudes are further removed from dehumanization than at least some ableist attitudes are, because there is a tendency to regard some disabled people as nonhuman, but the transgender person's humanity isn't in question. It's her gender that is. And to those people wedded to an essentialist conception of gender, she is experienced as a transgressive affront to the natural order. She then becomes the target of violence from those who wish to put her in what people regard as her "natural" gendered place.

26 | RESISTING

When I first set out to write this book I was a little worried about the subtitle. I was worried that readers might expect me to deliver some sort of tidy formula for getting rid of dehumanization. Resisting dehumanization is complicated, because dehumanization is complicated. It's not something that can be expressed in a set of bullet points or a list of rules.

I've assumed from the outset that resisting dehumanization has to be based on an understanding of how it works, and my main goal in writing this book has been to explain these things in the most accurate way that I can muster. In this, the concluding chapter, I want to distill and emphasize some key points about resisting dehumanization that I think are particularly important for you, the reader, to put into practice. I want this book to be one that you don't just read, but that you *use*.

Dehumanization is both political and psychological. It's about the distribution of power in the public sphere and it's about the beliefs that we form about ourselves and others. To resist dehumanization, you've got to understand how it works, and to understand how it works, you've got to understand both political and psychological aspects of it and how they interact. Insist on paying attention to both the political forces that push us to think of others as less than human and the psychological forces that make it possible for us to do so.

Resist dehumanization through political action and resist it by knowing yourself. Because dehumanization is produced by both political forces outside you and psychological processes within you, resisting dehumanization has to take place on two fronts. You can't combat the spread of dehumanizing beliefs without taking political action. At the very least you have to combat it in small ways in daily life, calling it out where you see it, objecting when people you speak to or people who represent you employ its dangerous rhetoric, and, crucially, opposing it in the voting booth. You may choose to oppose it in larger ways in the public sphere, making the decision to dedicate some or even most of your time to activism or politics to help be a force for good in the face of dehumanization's spread.

But to resist dehumanization you've also got to oppose the dehumanizing impulse in yourself. To do this, you need to understand that you are capable of dehumanizing others. Unless you accept this, and unless you are vigilant, you will be easy prey for dehumanizing propagandists. You will be more likely to be frightened by their xenophobic tales of bloodthirsty savages, and your tendency to essentialize others—which you share with the rest of humanity—may be triggered. People who dehumanize others aren't pure evil, or monsters, or animals, or scum. Thinking of them that way makes it hard for us to accept that we are all vulnerable to the dehumanizing impulse. So, *don't dehumanize the dehumanizers*. Doing that promotes the very attitude that you are trying to combat. People who dehumanize others are still people.

Try to think of them as people. Don't play their game, but don't delude yourself that you are not capable of playing it.

Don't confuse dehumanization with other kinds of bias. Dehumanization isn't the same as racism, anti-Semitism, sexism, objectification, religious bigotry, or prejudice against sexual minorities. All these things are bad, and all of them are dangerous, but dehumanization is potentially much more dangerous than the others. So, when you talk about dehumanization, try to be precise, rather than running lots of different things together. Remember, the word "dehumanization" has accumulated lots of different meanings, so don't assume that others know what you're talking about.

Study history to learn about dehumanization. Learn about genocide, colonialism, and racial oppression, and resist the temptation to think that we have put these things behind us. We haven't. Don't think of dehumanization as something that only other people do. It's easy to point to the crimes committed by others and to ignore or minimize the ones committed by those whom we consider our own. Learn the darkest history of your nation, religion, or ethnic group, and tell others what you have learned. Be brave and stand up for the truth. Stand up for humanity.

Know that dehumanization comes from outside of us. Human beings naturally tend to see others as human beings. The tendency to see them as subhuman creatures is foisted on us by people who have an investment in getting us to harm others. This implies that an important component of human nature is on our side in the struggle to resist dehumanization. Be wary of those who tell you that we are natural-born dehumanizers—that the urge to dehumanize others is in our genes. There's no reason to think that is the case. It may be true that human beings have an inherent disposition to be biased against outgroups, but outgroup bias is a far cry from dehumanization. And anyway, where the line gets drawn between ingroup and outgroup is a political matter. It's not something that's coded in our DNA.

Support a free press and freedom of speech. It's through media that dehumanizing ideas are spread and reproduced. That's why totalitarians puts a premium on destroying freedom of the press. Beware of attempts to destroy the credibility of media outlets that oppose and expose the dehumanizing propaganda of those in power. The Nazis referred to newspapers that opposed their message as the *Lügenpresse* (the "lying press") and claimed that it was run by Jews. In Myanmar, Wirathu and his followers claim that the media are against them because they're run by Muslims. Support the press. Subscribe to a newspaper. At least one.

Know that dehumanizing propaganda is usually not about hate. It's common to think of dehumanization as motivated by hate. This is a serious mistake. Dehumanizing propaganda trades mostly on desperation, fear, and the longing for salvation. Although it may feel good, calling people names and accusing them of hatefulness will not put an end to dehumanization. It will only make it stronger. The task of resisting dehumanization is too important for us not to be focused on what is most likely to get the best results. If you can, and if it is safe, treat your interlocuter as a human being. Try to have a conversation instead of trying to win a fight with them. It may prove impossible, at which point you'll have to walk away. But maybe even then you will have planted a seed of doubt in their mind that will grow into something more.

Remember that race is a social invention for justifying oppression.
Resisting race is crucial for resisting dehumanization, because as
long as racial categorizing persists, dehumanization is just around
the corner. Washing your hands of the concept of race is an act of
resistance and defiance. It doesn't mean that you are betraying your
family, your culture, or your history, or the work of securing justice
for racialized people, because it does not deny that people have
been treated as though race is real, and they have suffered from it.
Be prepared for negative reactions though. Others will resent you,
and they will try to put you back into the racial box, because you
are a threat to the whole hierarchical racial system. It's hard to resist the social and psychological pressures to embrace race, so try to
find like-minded people who will support you and whom you can
support. You may retort that this is easy for me, a White man, to
say. You'd be right. In most circumstances, I have the luxury of not
being racialized. But that observation only confirms my point that
race is by its very nature an oppressive ideology.

Following on from the previous point, *avoid using the words
"racist" and "racism" whenever possible.* Instead, be explicit about
what you mean. It's very easy for people to deny that they are racist,
but it's much harder for them to refute an explicit, clearly articu-
lated charge. When other people use these words, try to get them
to say what they mean by them. Racism isn't all about hate, so
don't use terms like "hate speech" and "hate group" as substitutes.
Concepts of race have racism built right into them, so know
that—like it or not—if you hold on to the concept of race, racism
will come along for the ride.

Know that almost any group can become racialized.
Dehumanization feeds on race. But race is not an objective

biological property of human beings; it's a social invention. People are racialized when they're regarded as an inferior natural human kind whose essence is transmitted by descent. That means that many different groups of people can become racialized. Ethnic groups, religious groups, national groups, and even political parties can become racialized, and, therefore, any of these can be dehumanized.

Know the warning signs. Although every episode of dehumanization is unique, they all have certain things in common. Know these signs, be alert to them, and call them out. It's usually the dominant group in a society that dehumanizes a vulnerable racialized minority and portrays themselves as victims of that minority. Notice when people in positions of power and influence—politicians, religious leaders, celebrities, and the like—say of others that they don't belong here, that they're not truly one of "us," and that they should go back to where they're "from" (even when they were born in the country where they are living). Listen closely for the language of parasitism—the charge that the despised minority are lazy (or as the Nazis put it, *arbeitssheu*—"work shy"), that they are sponging off conscientious, hard-working citizens, and that they have special privileges that the majority are denied. Be alert to statements or implications that a racial minority is essentially criminal, that they are breeding quickly and will soon overtake and replace the majority, and that they are dirty and diseased. Listen closely for animalistic slurs, and words like "predator," "infest," "infect," "poison," "breeding grounds," "invasion," "parasites," "swarm," and explicit or implicit comparisons of human beings with feces.

To conclude, it's important to be mindful of the fact that the scene of resistance is not always in the voting booth, on a protest march, or at the bully pulpit. Much—most—of our resistance is in everyday life. It's expressed in what we say and do at home with our children and spouses, at work with our colleagues, and at play with our friends. In all of these contexts, we can cumulatively affect the course of history, and work against the downward drag of the dehumanizing impulse. Martin Luther King Jr. once said, "The arc of history is long, but it bends toward justice." That's only half the story, because it only bends toward justice if we push it very hard to bend it that way.

NOTES

CHAPTER 2

1. Jean Hatzfeld, *Machete Season: The Killers in Rwanda Speak* (New York: Picador, 2005), 47, 144; Alison Liebhafsky Des Forges, *Leave None to Tell the Story: Genocide in Rwanda* (New York: Human Rights Watch, 1999), 347–348.
2. *New York Times*, January 9, 1943.
3. Michael C. C. Adams, "Retelling the Tale: Wars in Common Memory," in G. Boritt (Ed.), *War Comes Again: Comparative Vistas on the Civil War and World War II* (New York: Oxford University Press, 1995), 216.
4. Nick Turse, *Kill Anything That Moves: The Real American War in Vietnam* (New York: Picador, 2013), 50, 161.
5. Stan Goff, "Hold On to Your Humanity: An Open Letter to GIs in Iraq" (Southern Cross Review, 2007), https://southerncrossreview.org/31/goff.htm.

CHAPTER 4

1. Tom Segev, *Soldiers of Evil: The Commandants of the Nazi Concentration Camps* (New York: McGraw-Hill, 2007), 264.

CHAPTER 5

1. This figure is actually an underestimate, as an unknown (but very large) number of Mexicans and Native Americans were lynched in the western United States.
2. Christopher Waldrep, *Lynching in America: A History in Documents* (New York: New York University Press, 2006), 130–131.
3. W. E. B. Du Bois, *The Philadelphia Negro: A Social Study* (Philadelphia: University of Pennsylvania Press, 1995), 387.

CHAPTER 6

1. Dorothy Roberts, *Fatal Invention: How Science, Politics, and Big Business Re-create Race in the Twenty-first Century* (New York: New Press, 2012), 3.
2. L. Smith, *Killers of the Dream* (New York: Norton, 1994), 13–14.

CHAPTER 7

1. Rebecca Traister, "Our Racist History Isn't Back to Haunt Us. It Never Left Us," *New Republic* (June 18, 2015), https://newrepublic.com/article/122073/our-racial-history-isnt-back-haunt-us-it-never-left-us. This article is cited in Carlos Hoyt, *The Arc of a Bad Idea: Understanding and Transcending Race* (New York: Oxford University Press, 2016), which is an impassioned plea to leave the concept of race behind.
2. The text, in translation, can be found at "Himmler's Posen Speech— 'Extermination,'" Jewish Virtual Library, https://www.jewishvirtuallibrary.org/himmler-s-posen-speech-quot-extermination-quot. The sound recording, "Heinrich Himmler's Speech at Poznan," can be accessed on YouTube, https://www.youtube.com/watch?v=mRO04q_lQi4.
3. It's worth noting that oppressed people do not need to accept the illusion of race to reap these benefits. It is enough to unite under the banner of a *racialized* people.

CHAPTER 8

1. When I use the words "race" and "races," I mean the ordinary, vernacular conception rather than the way that these words might be understood by, say, population geneticists.

CHAPTER 9

1. With the exception of Reinhard Heydrich, members of the Nazi high command weren't especially Nordic-looking. Many of them could have easily passed as Jewish.
2. The second volume of Dixon's trilogy was the basis of the notorious film *The Birth of a Nation*, which contributed to the revival of the Ku Klux Klan in the early twentieth century.

CHAPTER 10

1. Malcolm X, *By Any Means Necessary: Malcolm X, Speeches and Writings* (New York: Pathfinder Press, 1992), 81.
2. Morgan Godwyn, *The Negro's and Indians Advocate Suing for Their Admission into the Church* (Whitefish, MT: Kessinger, 2001), 99.
3. Morgan Godwyn, *Trade Preferr'd before Religion and Christ Made to Give Place to Mammon Represented in a Sermon Relating to the Plantations: First Preached at Westminster-Abbey and Afterwards in Divers Churches in London* (printed for B. Took at the Ship in St. Paul's Church-yard, and for Isaac Cleave at the Star in Chancery-Lane, 1685).
4. Morgan Godwyn, "Neglect and Decay Thereof in Those Parts," in Francis Brokesby, *Some Proposals towards Promoting of the Gospel in Our American Plantations* (London: G. Sawbridge, 1708), 3.
5. Ibid.
6. "Der Untermensch" (The Subhuman), Holocaust Education and Archive Research Team, http://www.holocaustresearchproject.org/holoprelude/deruntermensch.html.

CHAPTER 12

1. T. J. Kasperbauer, *Subhuman: The Moral Psychology of Human Attitudes to Animals* (New York: Oxford University Press, 2018), 34.

CHAPTER 13

1. Helen Fein, *Accounting for Genocide: National Responses and Jewish Victimization during the Holocaust* (New York: Free Press, 1979), 4.
2. Claudia Koontz, *The Nazi Conscience* (Cambridge, MA: Harvard University Press, 2003), 3.
3. Richard Joyce, *The Evolution of Morality* (Cambridge, MA: MIT Press, 2007), 50.
4. Hannah Arendt, *Eichmann in Jerusalem: A Report on the Banality of Evil* (London: Penguin, 2006), 106.
5. Christopher Browning, *Ordinary Men: Reserve Police Battalion 101 and the Final Solution in Poland* (New York: HarperCollins, 1992), 69.

CHAPTER 14

1. Edward Westermann, "Stone-Cold Killers or Drunk with Murder? Alcohol and Atrocity during the Holocaust," *Holocaust and Genocide Studies* 30, no. 1 (2016): 2.
2. Simon Harrison, "The Symbolic Construction of Aggression and War in a Sepik River Society," *Man* 24, no. 4 (1989): 588.

CHAPTER 15

1. This is a deliberately oversimplified account of the evolution of bird wings. It's meant to illustrate a general point about how natural selection gives rise to functions, rather than capture the scientific details.
2. David Brion Davis, *Inhuman Bondage: The Rise and Fall of Slavery in the New World* (New York: Oxford University Press, 2006), 80.

CHAPTER 16

1. Claude Levi-Strauss, *Race and History* (New York: UNESCO, 1952), 12.

CHAPTER 17

1. Zsolt Bayer, "Who Should Not Be?" Orange Files, May 9, 2013, https://theorangefiles.hu/2013/05/09/who-should-not-be/.
2. Dehumanizing speech doesn't directly dehumanize people because, as I explained in chapter two, dehumanization is not a linguistic phenomenon. This form of speech dehumanizes indirectly, by causing others to adopt dehumanizing attitudes. The producer of the speech may or may not share these attitudes.
3. Miriam Eliav-Feldon, "Vagrants or Vermin? Attitudes towards Gypsies in Early Modern Europe," in M. Eliav-Feldon, I. Benjamin, and J. Ziegler (Eds.), *The Origins of Racism in the West* (Cambridge: Cambridge University Press, 2009), 290.
4. Adrian Bridge, "Romanians Vent Old Hatreds against Gypsies: The Villagers of Hadareni Are Defiant about Their Murder of Vermin," *Independent*, October 19, 1993, https://www.independent.co.uk/news/world/romanians-vent-old-hatreds-against-gypsies-the-villagers-of-hadareni-are-defiant-about-their-meurder-1511734.html.

CHAPTER 18

1. Sigmund Freud, "The Future of an Illusion," in *The Standard Edition of the Complete Psychological Works of Sigmund Freud, Vol. 21* (London: Hogarth Press and the Institute of Psycho-Analysis, 1964), 30.

2. Roger Money-Kyrle, "The Psychology of Propaganda," in *The Collected Papers of Roger Money-Kyrle* (London: Karnac, 2015), 165–166.

3. Ibid., 166.

4. "Donald Trump Transcript: 'Our Country Needs a Truly Great Leader,'" *Wall Street Journal*, June 16, 2015, http://blogs.wsj.com/washwire/2015/06/16/donald-trump-transcript-our-country-needs-a-truly-great-leader/.

5. Claudia Koonz, *The Nazi Conscience* (Cambridge, MA: Harvard University Press, 2003), 2.

CHAPTER 19

1. Jeffrey Gettleman, "Rohingya Recount Atrocities: 'They Threw My Baby into a Fire,'" *New York Times*, October 11, 2017, https://www.nytimes.com/2017/10/11/world/asia/rohingya-myanmar-atrocities.html?fbclid=IwAR2JE8IBfOYEGYYv4sPsSd3tfjBA7mawsYAzNPifwyqcDtzAcLEYqGlKG-E.

2. As I write this, he is a fugitive from justice, not because of his incitements to violence, but because of his criticism of the regime.

3. T. A. Kyau, "Buddhist Monk Wirathu Leads Violent National Campaign against Myanmar's Muslims," *GlobalPost*, June 21, 2013, https://www.pri.org/stories/2013-06-21/buddhist-monk-wirathu-leads-violent-national-campaign-against-myanmars-muslims.

4. Cited in Nicholas Gier, *The Origins of Religious Violence: An Asian Perspective* (London: Lexington Books, 2014), 67.

5. Thomas Fuller, "Extremism Rises among Myanmar Buddhists," *New York Times*, June 20, 2013, https://www.nytimes.com/2013/06/21/world/asia/extremism-rises-among-myanmar-buddhists-wary-of-muslim-minority.html.

6. C. J. Werleman, "Burma's 'Bin Laden' Compares Rohingya Muslims to Animals Who Eat with Their Asses," *Medium*, September 12, 2017.

7. Jonah Fisher, "Anti-Muslim Monk Stokes Burmese Religious Tension," *BBC News*, August 29, 2013, https://www.bbc.com/news/world-asia-23846632.

8. Patrick Winn, "Myanmar State Media Alludes to Rohingya Muslims as 'Human Fleas,'" *GlobalPost*, November 30, 2016, https://www.pri.org/stories/2016-11-30/myanmar-state-media-alludes-rohingya-muslims-human-fleas.

9. Steve Stecklow, "Why Facebook Is Losing the War on Hate Speech in Myanmar," *Reuters Investigates*, August 15, 2018.

10. Gettleman, "Rohingya Recount Atrocities."

11. Cited in "'*They Gave Them Long Swords*': *Preparations for Genocide and Crimes Against Humanity in Rakhine State, Myanmar,*" Fortify Rights [p. 97], July 2018.

12. Alex Preston, "The Rohingya and Myanmar's 'Buddhist Bin Laden,'" *GQ Magazine*, February 12, 2015, https://www.gq-magazine.co.uk/article/myanmar-rohingya-muslim-burma.

13. Hannah Beech, "The Face of Buddhist Terror," *Time*, July 1, 2013, http://content.time.com/time/subscriber/article/0,33009,2146000-2,00.html.

14. Francis Wade, "Wirathu, *Time* Magazine, and the Power of Propaganda in Burma," *Asian Correspondent*, June 25, 2013.

15. Kate Hodal, "Buddhist Monk Uses Racism and Rumours to Spread Hatred in Burma," *Guardian*, April 18, 2013, https://www.theguardian.com/world/2013/apr/18/buddhist-monk-spreads-hatred-burma.

16. "Report of the Independent International Fact-Finding Mission on Myanmar," Human Rights Council, September 12, 2018, https://www.ohchr.org/Documents/HRBodies/HRCouncil/FFM-Myanmar/A_HRC_39_64.pdf, 14.

17. Ibid., 15.

18. Matt Steib, "Everything We Know about Inhuman Conditions at Migrant Detention Camps," *New York Magazine* (July 20, 2019).

19. Anna Lind-Guzik, "I'm a Jewish Historian. Yes, We Should Call Border Detention Centers 'Concentration Camps,'" *Vox*, June 20, 2019, https://www.vox.com/first-person/2019/6/20/18693058/

aoc-alexandria-ocasio-cortez-concentration-camps-immigration-border.

CHAPTER 20

1. Cited in Robert Jan van Pelt, *Lodz and Getto Litzmannstadt: Promised Land and Croaking Hole of Europe* (Toronto: Art Gallery of Ontario, 2015), 36.
2. Joseph Goebbels, *Der Nazi-Sozi* (Elberfeld: Verlag der Nationalsozialistischen Briefe, 1927), https://research.calvin.edu/german-propaganda-archive/responses.htm.

CHAPTER 21

1. "The Eternal Jew," https://archive.org/details/TheEternalJewDerEwigeJude1940.
2. Mary Douglas, *Purity and Danger: An Analysis of the Concepts of Pollution and Taboo* (New York: Routledge, 2002).
3. You might be wondering why I don't also say that they could eliminate the contradiction by accepting that dehumanized people are fully human. This is possible in principle, but given the reasons why they're dehumanized in the first place, this isn't very likely.
4. Jews were forced to wear distinctive clothing—sometimes including a cloth badge—in the Middle Ages in parts of Christian Europe and the Muslim world. The Nazis revived this practice.
5. Cited in Orlando Patterson, *Rituals of Blood: Consequences of Slavery in Two American Centuries* (New York: Basic Books, 1998), 193.

CHAPTER 22

1. This is the testimony of Paul Mahehu, interviewed by Caroline Elkins, from her book *Imperial Reckoning: The Untold Story of Britain's Gulag in Kenya* (New York: Henry Holt and Company, 2005), 157.

2. Most people hear the words "concentration camp" with Hitler and the Nazis. But Hitler was a latecomer. He was inspired by the internment camps that the British set up in South Africa during the Boer War.

3. Caroline Elkins, *Imperial Reckoning: The Untold Story of Britain's Gulag in Kenya* (New York: Henry Holt and Company, 2005), 97.

4. In Daniel Jonah Goldhagen, *Worse Than War: Genocide, Eliminationism, and the Ongoing Assault on Humanity* (New York: Public Affairs, 2009), 327.

5. Cited in Barbara Higgs Strickland, *Saracens, Demons, Jews: Making Monsters in Medieval Art* (Princeton, NJ: Princeton University Press, 2003), 169.

6. Charles Smith, "Have American Negroes Too Much Liberty?" *Forum* (October 1893): 181; George Winston, "The Relations of the Whites to the Negroes," *Annals of the American Academy of Political and Social Science* 18 (1901): 108f.

7. Arthur Machen, *The House of Souls* (New York: Alfred A. Knopf, 1922), 116.

CHAPTER 23

1. H. R. Helper, *The Negroes in Negroland; the Negroes in America; and Negroes Generally. Also, the Several Races of White Men, Considered as the Involuntary and Predestined Supplanters of the Black Races* (New York: G. W. Carleton, 1868), 14, 244.

2. Cited in Grace Elizabeth Hale's *Making Whiteness: The Culture of Segregation in the South, 1890–1940* (New York: Vintage, 1999), 109.

3. Leonard Greene, "Trump Called for Death Penalty after Central Park Jogger Attack and Still Has No Sympathy for Accused Despite Convictions Overturned," *New York Daily News*, July 19, 2018 https://www.nydailynews.com/new-york/ny-news-trump-death-penalty-central-park-five-20180713-story.html.

4. Patrick Buchanan, "The Barbarians Are Winning," *New York Post*, April 30, 1989.

5. Dareh Gregorian, "Trump Digs In on Central Park 5: 'They Admitted Their Guilt,'" *NBC News*, June 18, 2019.

6. G. Bruney, "Breaking Down Donald Trump's Deranged Involvement in the Central Park Five Case," *Esquire*, May 26, 2019, https://www.esquire.com/entertainment/a27586174/when-they-see-us-central-park-5-donald-trump/.

7. "'I Can Be More Presidential Than Any President.' Read Trump's Ohio Rally Speech," *Time*, July 26, 2017, http://time.com/4874161/donald-trump-transcript-youngstown-ohio/.

8. A. Waytz, K. M. Hoffman, and S. Trawalter, "A Superhumanization Bias in Whites' Perceptions of Blacks," *Social Psychological and Personality Science* 6, no. 3 (2015): 352–359.

9. A. Waytz, K. M. Hoffman, and S. Trawalter, "The Racial Bias Embedded in Darren Wilson's Testimony," *Washington Post* (November 26, 2014). The authors go on to remark that in one of their studies, "whites were particularly adept at processing a set of words including Wilson's depiction, demon, when a black face appeared on the computer screen just before." Needless to say, whether or not this conjecture is correct has no bearing on the guilt or innocence of Darren Wilson, whom the grand jury acquitted.

10. M. Berkowitz, *The Crime of My Very Existence: Nazism and the Myth of Jewish Criminality* (Berkeley: University of California Press, 2007), 48.

11. Quoted in A. G. Hardy, *Hitler's Secret Weapon: The "Managed" Press and Propaganda Machine of Nazi Germany* (New York: Vantage, 1967), 197.

CHAPTER 24

1. Kwame Anthony Appiah, *Experiments in Ethics* (Cambridge, MA: Harvard University Press, 2010), 144.

2. Stanley Elkins, *Slavery: A Problem in American Institutional and Intellectual Life* (Chicago: University of Chicago Press, 1976), 82.

3. T. Snyder, *Black Earth: The Holocaust as History and Warning* (New York: Tim Duggan Books, 2015).

4. Quoted in D. E. Stannard, *American Holocaust: The Conquest of the New World* (New York: Oxford University Press, 1992), 245.

CHAPTER 25

1. John Hagan and Wenona Rymond-Richmond, "The Collective Dynamics of Racial Dehumanization and Genocidal Victimization in Darfur," *American Sociological Review* 73 (2008): 875–902.

2. C. A. MacKinnon, *Are Women Human? and Other International Dialogues* (Cambridge, MA: Harvard University Press, 2006), 4.

READING DEEPER

This book is the result of more than a decade of research. I've tried to make it as accessible as possible, and to avoid burdening the text (and the reader!) with scholarly references and arcane terminology, as far as this was possible. However, I'm also aware that some readers may want to check whether I've gotten my facts right, and may also want to explore more deeply some of the topics that I've raised. So, I include here a chapter-by-chapter collection of readings. It consists mainly of texts that I've found to be particularly helpful, and which I would recommend to anyone wishing to find out more. This list isn't meant to be comprehensive, but for readers who look forward to exploring dehumanization in greater depth, the material here will help to provide a solid foundation.

ONE: INTRODUCTION

My book *Less Than Human: Why We Demean, Enslave, and Exterminate Others* (New York: St. Martin's Press, 2011) provides a wealth of information on the history of dehumanization and how it should be understood. A summary appeared in *Aeon* magazine as "The Essence of Evil," which can be accessed at https://aeon.co/essays/why-is-it-so-easy-to-dehumanise-a-victim-of-violence. My forthcoming book *Making Monsters: The Uncanny Power of Dehumanization* (Cambridge, MA: Harvard University Press) will be an excellent companion to the present text. There are more resources on dehumanization and related topics at my website, http://www.davidlivingstonesmith.com.

TWO: WHY DEHUMANIZATION MATTERS

Marjorie Spiegel's *The Dreaded Comparison: Human and Animal Slavery* (New York: Mirror Books, 1996) is packed with examples and is short enough to be read in a single sitting. For information on dehumanization in the Rwanda genocide, see Jean Hatzfeld's *Machete Season: The Killers in Rwanda Speak* (New York: Picador, 2006). For dehumanization in genocide more generally, see Daniel Jonah Goldhagen's *Worse Than War: Genocide, Eliminationism, and the Ongoing Assault on Humanity* (New York: Public Affairs, 2009). For a more technical discussion that repays careful attention, I strongly recommend Lynne Tirrell's "Genocidal Language Games," in Ishani Maitra and Mary Kate McGowan (Eds.), *Speech and Harm: Controversies over Free Speech* (New York: Oxford University Press, 2012). There is shockingly little literature on the dehumanization of enslaved people in the United States, and David Brion Davis's *The Problem of Slavery in the Age of Emancipation* (New York: Penguin Random House, 2015) is one of the few discussions of this topic. Sam Keen's *Faces of the Enemy: Reflections of the Hostile Imagination* (New York: Harper and Row, 1991) is worthwhile for the illustrations of dehumanizing visual propaganda alone. John Dower's *War without Mercy: Race and Power in the Pacific War* (New York: Pantheon, 1987) is a classic study of the role of racism, and, to some extent, dehumanization, in the Pacific theater of World War II. For the go-to source on dehumanizing media coverage of America's recent wars (including the "war on terror"), see Erin Steuter and Deborah Wills, *At War with Metaphor: Media, Propaganda, and Racism in the War on Terror* (Lanham, MD: Lexington Books, 2009). The best source on the Munducuru is Robert Murphy's classic "Intergroup Hostility and Social Cohesion," *American Anthropologist* 59 (1957): 1018–1035.

THREE: DEFINING DEHUMANIZATION

For early history of the concept of dehumanization, from ancient times to the present, see my *Less Than Human: Why We Demean, Enslave, and Exterminate Others* (New York: St Martin's Press, 2011). Two classic early treatments of the topic of dehumanization by psychologists are Herbert C. Kelman's "Violence without Moral Restraint: Reflections on the Dehumanization of Victims and Victimizers," *Journal of Social Issues* 29, no. 4 (1973): 25–61); and Albert Bandura, Bill Underwood, and Michael E. Fromson's "Disinhibition of Aggression through Diffusion of Responsibility and Dehumanization of Victims," *Journal of Research in Personality* 9 (1975): 253–269. Social psychologists have produced an extensive literature on dehumanization since the late 1990s. A good entry point into this is the volume edited by Paul Bain, Jerome Vaes, and Jacques-Philippe Leyens entitled *Humanness and Dehumanization* (New York: Routledge, 2013). Nick Haslam is by far the most influential and prolific psychological theorist of dehumanization. For a good introduction to his views, consult his article co-authored with Steve Loughnan, "Dehumanization and Infrahumanization," *Annual Review of Psychology* 65 (2014): 399–423; and his "Dehumanization: An Integrative Review," *Personality and Social Psychology Review* 10, no. 3 (2006): 252–264. For criticisms of some of the mainstream social psychological approaches, see my "Dehumanization, Essentialism, and Moral Psychology," *Philosophy Compass* 9, no. 11 (2014): 914–924. And for contributions on the topic by feminist philosophers, see Linda Lemoncheck's *Dehumanizing Women: Treating Persons as Sex Objects* (New York: Rowman and Littlefield, 1985); Mari Mikkola's *The Wrong of Injustice: Dehumanization and Its Role in Feminist Philosophy* (Oxford, UK: Oxford University Press, 2016); and Kate Manne's *Down Girl: The Logic of Misogyny* (New York: Oxford University Press, 2017).

FOUR: HOLOCAUST

There are numerous excellent works on the history of Christian anti-Semitism. I particularly recommend Debra Higgs Strickland's beautifully illustrated *Saracens, Demons, and Jews: Making Monsters in Medieval Art* (Princeton, NJ: Princeton University Press, 2003), and William Nichols's *Christian Antisemitism: A History of Hate* (Lanham, MD: Jason Aronson, 1993). Three good books on the history of anti-Semitism from ancient times to the present are Marvin Perry and Frederick M. Schweitzer's *Antisemitic Myths: A Historical and Contemporary Anthology* (Bloomington: Indiana University Press, 2008); Robert S. Wistrich's *A Lethal Obsession: Anti-Semitism from Antiquity to the Global Jihad* (New York: Random House, 2010); and David Nirenberg's *Anti-Judaism: The History of a Way of Thinking* (New York: W. W. Norton, 2013). For a penetrating study of the role of dehumanization in Nazi ideology, see Johannes Steizinger's "The Significance of Dehumanization: Nazi Ideology and Its Psychological Consequences," *Politics, Religion, and Ideology*

19, no. 1 (2018): 1–19. There is a fascinating discussion of the *Judensau* image in Isaiah Sachar, *The Judensau: A Medieval Anti-Jewish Motif and Its History* (London: Warburg Institute, 1974). The best source for the American influence on Nazi race laws is James Q. Whitman's *Hitler's American Model: The United States and the Making of Nazi Race Law* (Princeton, NJ: Princeton University Press, 2017). Finally, I strongly recommend Claudia Koonz, *The Nazi Conscience* (Cambridge, MA: Harvard University Press, 2005), for a study of the role of race and racism in the Nazi worldview.

FIVE: LYNCHING

There are a number of superb books on the history of lynching. For general introductions, I particularly recommend Philip Dray's *At the Hands of Persons Unknown: The Lynching of Black America* (New York: Modern Library, 2002); and Leon F. Litwack's *Trouble in Mind: Black Southerners in the Age of Jim Crow* (New York: Vintage, 1998). Christopher Waldrep's edited volume *Lynching in America: A History in Documents* (New York: New York University Press, 2006) is a compendium of primary sources; and Ralph Ginzburg's *100 Years of Lynchings* (Baltimore: Black Classics Press, 1962) consists entirely of newspaper articles on lynchings and other forms of violence against Black people, from 1880 to 1961. Two books about ethnic cleansing in the United States that should not be missed are Patrick Phillips's *Blood at the Root: A Racial Cleansing in America* (New York: W. W. Norton, 2016); and Elliot Jaspin's *Buried in the Bitter Waters: The Hidden History of Racial Cleansing in America* (New York: Basic Books, 2008). Grace Elizabeth Hale's magnificent *Making Whiteness: The Culture of Segregation in the South, 1890–1940* (New York: Vintage, 1999) is an indispensable resource that discusses the Neal lynching, as well as others cited in this book. Another crucial resource on lynching is Amy Louise Wood's *Lynching and Spectacle: Witnessing Racial Violence in America, 1890–1940* (Chapel Hill: University of North Carolina Press, 2009)—an extremely important contribution to the literature on lynching. For a fascinating analysis of lynching as a ritual of human sacrifice, Orlando Patterson's essay "Feast of Blood," in his *Rituals of Blood: Consequences of Slavery in Two American Centuries* (New York: Basic Books, 1998). Ida

B. Wells was a brilliant and brave campaigner against lynching in the United States, and it's well worth reading her biography by Paula J. Giddings, *Ida: A Sword among Lions—Ida B. Wells and the Campaign against Lynching* (New York: Amistad, 2009). There are two books specifically about the Claude Neal lynching. I recommend James R. McGovern's *Anatomy of a Lynching: The Killing of Claude Neal* (Baton Rouge: University of Louisiana Press, 1982). The other book, Dale Cox's self-published *The Claude Neal Lynching: The 1934 Murders of Claude Neal and Lola Canady* (Bascomb, FL: Old Kitchen Books, 2012), should be treated with caution. It comes across as an apology for the Jim Crow South, but it also contains some very interesting oral history. For a sophisticated, historically informed discussion of the construction of Black masculinity that is relevant to the topic of lynching, I strongly recommend Tommy J. Curry, *The Man Not: Race, Class, Genre, and the Dilemmas of Black Manhood* (Philadelphia: Temple University Press, 2017).

SIX: HOW WE DO RACE

For an introduction to differing views about what race is, get your hands on a copy of Albert Atkin's *Philosophy of Race* (New York: Routledge, 2014); or Paul C. Taylor's *Race: A Philosophical Introduction* (Malden, MA: Polity Press, 2013). There is a good, clear discussion of races as natural kinds in Alyssa Ney's *Metaphysics: An Introduction* (New York: Routledge, 2014). For why there are no human subspecies, see Adam Hochman's "Against the New Racial Naturalism," *Journal of Philosophy* 110, no. 6 (2013): 331–351. For an accessible discussion of race as fictional, have a look at Carlos A. Hoyt's *The Arc of a Bad Idea: Understanding and Transcending Race* (Oxford, UK: Oxford University Press, 2016). Four philosophers with sharply divergent views about the reality of race have written a book in which they thrash out the issues: G. Glasgow, S. Haslanger, C. Jeffers, and Q. Spencer, *What Is Race? Four Philosophical Views* (New York: Oxford University Press, 2019). From a more sociological angle, Ann Morning's *The Nature of Race: How Scientists Think and Teach about Human Difference* (Los Angeles: University of California Press, 2011) repays close attention. For the ancestral pedigrees of Jews during the Nazi era, see Eric Ehrenreich, *The Nazi Ancestral Proof: Genealogy, Racial Science, and the*

Final Solution (Bloomington: Indiana University Press, 2007). Two fine books that deal with the history of racial passing are Daniel Scharfstein's *The Invisible Line: A Secret History of Race in America* (New York: Penguin, 2011); and Allyson Hobbs, *A Chosen Exile: A History of Racial Passing in American Life* (Cambridge, MA: Harvard University Press, 2014).

SEVEN: RACISM

There is a substantial literature on the nature of racism. For a compelling history painted in broad brushstrokes, I recommend Ibram X. Kendi's *Stamped from the Beginning: The Definitive History of Racist Ideas in America* (New York: Nation Books, 2016). Albert Atkin surveys views on the nature of racism in *The Philosophy of Race* (New York: Routledge, 2014). Important and accessible philosophical contributions to the analysis of racism include Kwame Anthony Appiah's "Racisms," in David Goldberg's *Anatomy of Racism* (Minneapolis: University of Minnesota Press, 1990); Jorge Garcia's "The Heart of Racism," *Journal of Social Philosophy* 27, no. 1 (1996): 5–46; and Lawrence Blum's "Racism: What It Is and What It Isn't," *Studies in Philosophy and Education* 21, no. 3 (2002): 203–218. The classic text on structural racism is Edouardo Bonilla-Silva's *Racism without Racists: Color-Blind Racism and the Persistence of Racial Inequality in America* (New York: Rowman and Littlefield, 2009). A really good paper on Aristotle's theory of natural slavery is Malcolm Heath's "Aristotle on Natural Slavery," *Phronesis: A Journal for Ancient Philosophy* 53, no. 3 (2008): 243–270. Siep Stuurman has a fine discussion of the Spanish Colonists' appropriation of Aristotle's thesis in *The Invention of Humanity: Equality and Cultural Difference in World History* (Cambridge, MA: Harvard University Press, 2017). Lewis Hanke's *All Mankind Is One* (DeKalb: Southern Illinois University Press, 1974) is all about the debate between las Casas and Sepúlveda.

EIGHT: RACE SCIENCE

Jon Marks's *Is Science Racist?* (London: Polity, 2017) is a short, engaging introduction to the history of how racist ideology deforms science. For an account of the return of scientific racism, I recommend science journalist Angela

Saini's *Superior: The Return of Race Science* (Boston: Beacon Press, 2019); and for the persistence of outmoded racial ideas in biomedical science, see Dorothy Roberts's *Fatal Invention: How Science, Politics, and Big Business Re-create Race in the Twenty-first Century* (New York: New Press, 2012). The original groundbreaking paper by Rosenberg and his colleagues is Noah A. Rosenberg, Jonathan K. Pritchard, James L. Weber, Howard M. Cann, Kenneth K. Kidd, Lev A. Zhivotovsky and Marcus W. Feldman's "Genetic Structure of Human Populations," *Science* 298 (2002): 2381–2385. Melissa Wills takes on misinterpretations of the STRUCTURE results in her "Are Clusters Races? A Discussion of the Rhetorical Appropriation of Rosenberg et al.'s 'Genetic Structure of Human Populations,'" *Philosophy, Theory, and Practice in Biology* 9, no. 12 (2017), http://dx.doi.org/10.3998/ptb.6959004.0009.012. Other penetrating discussions include Massimo Pigliucci's "What Are We to Make of the Concept of Race? Thoughts of a Philosopher-Scientist," *Studies in History and Philosophy of Biological and Biomedical Science* 44 (2017): 272–277; and his paper co-authored with Jonathan Kaplan, "On the Concept of Biological Race and Its Applicability to Humans," *Philosophy of Science* 70 (2003): 1161–1171.

NINE: ESSENCE

There is quite a large and growing literature on psychological essentialism. Paul Bloom's *How Pleasure Works: The New Science of Why We Like What We Like* (New York: W. W. Norton, 2011) is a great introduction to psychological essentialism. Susan Gelman's *The Essential Child: Origins of Essentialism in Everyday Thought* (New York: Oxford University Press, 2003) is a valuable resource on the developmental psychology of essentialist cognition. Lawrence A. Hirshfeld's *Race in the Making: Cognition, Culture, and the Child's Construction of Human Kinds* (Cambridge, MA: MIT Press, 1998) is a pioneering study of the development of racial essentialism in children. For an up-to-date discussion of the role of psychological essentialism in racial cognition, consult Luc Faucher's chapter "Biophilosophy of Race," in D. L. Smith (Ed.), *How Biology Shapes Philosophy: New Foundations for Naturalism* (Cambridge, UK: Cambridge University Press, 2017). Finally, my two all-time favorite articles on psychological essentialism are Sarah-Jane Leslie's "Essence and Natural

Kinds: When Science Meets Preschooler Intuition," in T. S. Gendler and J. Hawthorne (Eds.), *Oxford Studies in Epistemology, Vol. 4* (Oxford, UK: Oxford University Press, 2013); and Paul E. Griffiths's "What is Innateness?" *Monist* 85, no. 1 (2001): 70–85. Daniel Chirot and Clark McCauley discuss essentialism in genocide in *Why Not Kill Them All? The Logic and Prevention of Mass Political Murder* (Princeton, NJ: Princeton University Press, 2006).

TEN: FROM BARBADOS TO NAZI GERMANY

A facsimile edition of Godwyn's most important work is *The Negro's & Indians Advocate, Suing for Their Admission to the Church* (Whitefish, MT: Kessinger, 2010). For biographical information on Godwyn, a good source is A. T. Vaughan, *Roots of American Racism: Essays on the Colonial Experience* (New York: Oxford University Press, 2005). *Der Untermensch* can be found online at the Holocaust Education & Archive Research Team site, http://www. holocaustresearchproject.org/holoprelude/deruntermensch.html.

ELEVEN: WHICH LIVES MATTER?

Arthur O. Lovejoy's *The Great Chain of Being: A Study of the History of an Idea* (Cambridge, MA: Harvard University Press, 1942) is the *locus classicus* for the concept of the Great Chain of Being. One of the very few works on the psychology of hierarchical thinking is T. J. Kasperbauer's *Subhuman: The Moral Psychology of Human Attitudes to Animals* (New York: Oxford University Press, 2018). The philosopher Bernard Williams offers an attempted justification for the attitude of granting human beings privileged moral status in "The Human Prejudice," in B. Williams, *Philosophy as a Humanistic Discipline* (Princeton, NJ: Princeton University Press, 2006). For a nice sampling of pertinent articles, check out Raymond Corbey and Annette Lanjouw's edited volume *The Politics of Species: Reshaping Our Relationships with Other Animals* (Cambridge, UK: Cambridge University Press, 2013). For a study of attempts to draw a hierarchical line between humans and "lower" primates, see Raymond Corbey's *The Metaphysics of Apes: Negotiating the Animal-Human Boundary* (Cambridge, UK: Cambridge University Press, 2005).

TWELVE: THE ACT OF KILLING

Bernard V. Verkamp's book *The Moral Treatment of Returning Warriors in Early Medieval and Modern Times* (Scranton, NJ: University of Scranton Press, 2006) is a detailed study of the medieval Christian view that the act of killing stains the soul. My paper, co-authored with Ioana Panaitiu, entitled "Horror Sanguinis," *Common Knowledge* 22, no. 1 (2016): 69–80 is a cross-cultural and transhistorical study of the belief that the act of killing contaminates the killer. Rachel M. MacNair discusses psychiatric harm induced by killing in *Perpetration-Induced Traumatic Stress: The Psychological Consequences of Killing* (New York: Praeger, 2002); and in *Psychology of Peace: An Introduction* (New York: Praeger, 2012). Finally, there is Randall Collins's encyclopedic study of the human aversion to violence: *Violence: A Micro-Sociological Theory* (Princeton, NJ: Princeton University Press, 2008). For an experimental study of the reluctance to physically harm others, go to Fiery Cushman, Kurt Gray, Allison Gaffey, and Wendy Berry Mendes's "Simulating Murder: The Aversion to Harmful Action," *Emotion* 12, no. 1 (2012): 2–7. In this connection, see also Gina Perry's page-turning investigation into the Milgram obedience experiments in *Behind the Shock Machine: The Untold Story of the Notorious Milgram Psychology Experiments* (New York: New Press, 2012).

THIRTEEN: MORALITY

For dehumanization as a form of moral disengagement, see Albert Bandura's "Moral Disengagement in the Perpetration of Inhumanities," *Personality and Social Psychology Review* 3, no. 3 (1999): 193–209. The view that violence tends to be moralistic is well developed in Alan Fiske and Tage Rai's *Virtuous Violence: Hurting and Killing to Create, Sustain, End, and Honor Social Relationships* (Cambridge, UK: Cambridge University Press, 2014). Richard Joyce distinguishes between inhibitions and prohibitions in *The Evolution of Morality* (Cambridge, MA: MIT Press, 2007). For Eichmann, see Bettina Stangneth's *Eichmann before Jerusalem: The Unexamined Life of a Mass Murderer* (New York: Alfred A. Knopf, 2014). David Grossman's *On Killing* (Boston: Little, Brown and Company, 1995) discusses how soldiers morally disengage. For moral distancing in genocide, Z. Bauman's *Modernity and the Holocaust* (Ithaca, NY: Cornell University Press, 1989) is an important source.

FOURTEEN: SELF-ENGINEERING

The best source on the use of drugs in combat is Lukasz Kamienski's *Shooting Up: A History of Drugs in Warfare* (London: C. Hurst, 2017). The anthropologist Paul Roscoe describes methods that humans have developed to disable inhibitions against violence in his paper "Intelligence, Coalitional Killing, and the Antecedents of War," *American Anthropologist* 109 (2007): 485–495. David Grossman's *On Killing: The Psychological Cost of Learning to Kill in War and Society* (Boston: Little, Brown and Company, 1995) is highly accessible and has been very influential. Grossman draws on S. L. A. Marshall's controversial classic *Men against Fire: The Problem of Battle Command in Future War* (New York: William Morrow, 1947), a foundational text in this literature. For music as an aid to dissociation in combat, see Jonathan Pieslak's *Sound Targets: American Soldiers and Music in the Iraq War* (Bloomington: Indiana University Press, 2009). For thoughts on good and bad forms of dehumanization in combat, see Shannon French and Anthony Jack's "Dehumanizing the Enemy: The Intersection of Neuroethics and Military Ethics," in D. Whetham and B. J. Strawser (Eds.), *Responsibilities to Protect: Perspective in Theory and Practice* (Leiden, The Netherlands: Brill Nijhoff, 2015).

FIFTEEN: IDEOLOGY

There is a sprawling literature in philosophy and the social sciences on the topic of ideology. The theory of ideology presented in the volume is described in greater depth in my chapter "How Media Makes, Ignites, and Breaks Ideology," in C. Fox and J. Saunders (Eds.), *Media Ethics, Free Speech, and the Requirements of Democracy* (London: Routledge, 2019). There is a good deal of disagreement about what ideology is. John Gerring's article "Ideology: A Definitional Analysis," *Political Research Quarterly* 50, no. 4 (1997): 957–994, and Terry Eagleton's book *Ideology: An Introduction* (London: Verso, 2007) are enlightening surveys of the conceptual landscape. Raymond Geuss's *The Idea of a Critical Theory: Habermas and the Frankfurt School* (Cambridge,

UK: Cambridge University Press, 1981) is a classic. Karl Marx's writings are the point of departure for most work on ideology, but there is considerable disagreement about what Marx's conception of ideology actually was. Joseph McCarney's *The Real World of Ideology* (London: Harvester, 1980) offers a careful and lucid exegesis of Marx's viewpoint. Finally, two important articles on ideology by contemporary philosophers are Sally Haslanger's "Culture and Critique," *Proceedings of the Aristotelian Society Supplementary* 91, no. 1 (2017): 149–173; and Tommy Shelby's "Ideology, Racism, and Critical Social Theory," *Philosophical Forum* 34, no. 2 (2003): 153–188.

SIXTEEN: THE POLITICS OF THE HUMAN

For Mayr's account of bird taxonomy, see his *Animal Species and Evolution* (Cambridge, MA: Harvard University Press, 1963). For the Karam, go to Ralph Bulmer's "Why Is the Cassowary Not a Bird? A Problem of Zoological Taxonomy among the Karam of the New Guinea Highlands," *Man* 2 (1967): 5–25. For views of humanness similar to my own, see Ann Phillips's *The Politics of the Human* (Cambridge, UK: Cambridge University Press, 2015); and Michael Hauskeller's "Making Sense of What We Are: A Mythological Approach to Human Nature," *Philosophy* 4 (2009): 95–109. You can also consult my article "Indexically Yours: Why Being Human Is More Like Being Here Than Like Being Water," in R. Corbey and A. Lanjouw (Eds.), *The Politics of Species: Reshaping Our Relationships with Other Animals* (Cambridge, UK: Cambridge University Press, 2013). For hypersociality, go to E. O. Wilson's *The Social Conquest of the Earth* (New York: Liveright, 2013); Mark Moffett's *The Human Swarm: How Societies Arise, Thrive, and Fall* (New York: Basic Books, 2019); and Michael Tomasello's "The Ultra-Social Animal," *European Journal of Social Psychology* 44, no. 3 (2014): 187–194.

SEVENTEEN: DANGEROUS SPEECH

For more information on Bayer's dehumanizing rhetoric, see "Zsolt Bayer, the Purveyor of Hate, in His Own Words," Hungarian Spectrum, https:// hungarianspectrum.org/2016/08/19/zsolt-bayer-the-purveyor-of-hate-in-his-own-words/; and Kata Karáth's "All of a Sudden, Nobody Wants One of

Hungary's Highest National Honors," *Quartz*, September 9, 2016, https://qz.com/774556/all-of-a-sudden-nobody-wants-one-of-hungarys-highest-national-honors/. For a superb discussion of propaganda, go to Jason Stanley's *How Propaganda Works* (Princeton, NJ: Princeton University Press, 2015). Victor Klemperer's *The Language of the Third Reich* (London: Bloomsbury Revelations, 2013) is a classic discussion of Nazi propaganda. Another very useful book on Nazi propaganda is Randall L. Bytwerk's *Bending Spines: The Propagandas of Nazi Germany and the German Democratic Republic* (East Lansing: University of Michigan Press, 2004). Other important contributions are C. C. Aronsfeld's *The Text of the Holocaust: A Study of the Nazis' Extermination Propaganda, 1919–1945* (Marblehead, MA: Micah Publications, 1985); and Felicity Rash's *The Language of Violence: Adolf Hitler's Mein Kampf* (New York: Peter Lang, 2006). Jeffery Herf's book *The Jewish Enemy: Nazi Propaganda during World War II and the Holocaust* (Cambridge, MA: Harvard University Press, 2006) is another great resource. For dangerous speech, see Jonathan Leader Maynard and Susan Benesch's "Dangerous Speech and Dangerous Ideology: An Integrated Model for Monitoring and Prevention," *Genocide Studies and Prevention* 9, no. 3 (2016): 71–95; Shantal Marshall's "When 'Scurry' vs. 'Hurry' Makes the Difference: Vermin Metaphors, Disgust, and Anti-Immigrant Attitudes," *Journal of Social Issues* 74, no. 4 (2018): 774–789; and Erin Steuter and Deborah Wills's *At War with Metaphor: Media, Propaganda, and Racism in the War on Terror* (New York: Rowman and Littlefield, 2018). For Goebbels's speech at the unveiling of the "people's receiver," go to "The Radio as the Eight Great Power," German Propaganda Archive, https://research.calvin.edu/german-propaganda-archive/goeb56.htm.

EIGHTEEN: ILLUSION

Jason Stanley's *How Fascism Works: The Politics of Us and Them* (New York: Random House, 2018) is a very readable book, providing a framework for understanding authoritarian propaganda. There are very good discussions of Freud's theory of illusion in Benjamin Beit-Hallami's *Psychoanalysis and Theism: Critical Reflections on the Grünbaum Thesis*

(New York: Jason Aronson, 2010). For Money-Kyrle's paper, go to *The Collected Papers of Roger Money-Kyrle* (London: Karnac, 2015). The journalist Gwynn Guilford attended Trump rallies and tested my claim that Trump follows the rhetorical pattern described by Money-Kyrle. Read her conclusions in "Inside the Trump Machine: The Bizarre Psychology of America's Newest Political Movement," *Quartz*, April 1, 2016, https://qz.com/645345/inside-the-trump-machine-the-bizarre-psychology-of-americas-newest-political-movement/. My essay in *Aeon* entitled "Why We Love Tyrants" discusses political propaganda from the perspectives of Socrates, Freud, and Money-Kyrle, https://aeon.co/essays/the-omnipotent-victim-how-tyrants-work-up-a-crowds-devotion.

NINETEEN: GENOCIDE

The dehumanization of the Rohingya is bound up with the long, complex history of Myanmar. Works that I have found to be particularly informative are the Fortify Rights report entitled "'They Gave Them Long Swords': Preparations for Genocide and Crimes against Humanity against Rohingya Muslims in Rakhine State,"

https://humanrightscommission.house.gov/sites/humanrightscommission.house.gov/files/documents/Fortify_Rights_Long_Swords_July_2018.pdf; Azeem Ibrahim's *The Rohingyas: Inside Myanmar's Genocide* (London: C. Hurst, 2016); Matt Schissler, Matthew J. Walton, and Phyu Phyu Thi's "Threat and Virtuous Defense: Listening to Narratives of Religious Conflict in Six Myanmar Cities," St. Anthony's College, https://www.sant.ox.ac.uk/sites/default/files/m.mas_working_paper_1.1_-_threat_and_virtuous_defence_-_july_2015.pdf; and the United Nations Human Rights Council's report "Independent International Fact-Finding Mission on Myanmar," https://www.ohchr.org/en/hrbodies/hrc/myanmarffm/pages/index.aspx.

TWENTY: CONTRADICTION

For a superb account of the Lodz ghetto, check out Robert Jan van Pelt's *Lodz and Getto Litzmannstadt: Promised Land and Croaking Hole of Europe* (Toronto: Art Gallery of Ontario, 2015). For a readable introduction to the debate that has been swirling around the concept of dehumanization, a good place to start is Paul Bloom's "The Root of All Cruelty?" in November 20, 2017, issue of the *New Yorker*. In the article, Bloom discusses the differences between my realist view of dehumanization and the more skeptical position advanced by Cornell University philosopher Kate Manne in her book *Down Girl: The Logic of Misogyny* (New York: Oxford University Press, 2017). For my initial response to Manne, see my "Paradoxes of Dehumanization," *Social Theory and Practice* 42, no. 2 (2016): 416–443. For two critical philosophical engagements with Manne's account of dehumanization, see Ishani Maitra's "Misogyny and Humanism"; and Audrey Yap's "Misogyny and Dehumanization," in the Spring 2019 issue of the American Philosophical Association's *Newsletter on Feminist Philosophy*, together with Manne's responses. Manne's critique of the concept of dehumanization was preceded by Adam Gopnik, in "Headless Horsemen: The Reign of Terror Revisited," *New Yorker* (June 5, 2006); Kwame Anthony Appiah in his *Experiments in Ethics* (Cambridge, MA: Harvard University Press, 2010); and Johannes Lang's "Questioning Dehumanization: Intersubjective Dimensions of Violence in the Nazi Concentration and Death Camps," *Holocaust and Genocide Studies* 24, no. 2 (2016): 225–246.

TWENTY-ONE: IMPURITY

The Eternal Jew can be accessed online at https://archive.org/details/TheEternalJewDerEwigeJude1940. There are interesting discussions of the film in Robert Jan van Pelt's *Lodz and Getto Litzmannstadt: Promised Land and Croaking Hole of Europe* (Toronto: Art Gallery of Ontario, 2015); and Richard Taylor's *Film Propaganda: Soviet Russia and Nazi Germany* (London: I. B. Taurus, 2006). The Danish scholar Stig Hornshøj-Møller has studied the film, and argues that it was, in effect, an order for genocide. You can find links to his papers at the Holocaust History Project, https://phdn.org/archives/holocaust-history.org/der-ewige-jude/index.html. The classic source on impurity is Mary Douglas's *Purity and Danger: An Analysis of Concepts of Pollution and Taboo* (New York: Routledge, 2002). There is a large literature now on disgust, which most authors link to impurity; see Daniel Kelly's *Yuck! The Nature and Moral Significance of Disgust* (Cambridge, MA: MIT Press, 2011); and William Ian Miller's *The Anatomy of Disgust* (Cambridge, MA: Harvard University Press,

1997). For spectacle lynchings, including the lynching of Henry Smith, Amy Louise Woods's *Lynching and Spectacle: Witnessing Racial Violence in America, 1890–1940* (Chapel Hill: University of North Carolina Press, 2009) is an indispensable resource.

TWENTY-TWO: MONSTERS

Noël Carroll's *The Philosophy of Horror: or, Paradoxes of the Heart* (New York: Routledge, 2015) is a compelling analysis. Carroll's account of monsters is grounded in anthropologist Mary Douglas's influential book *Purity and Danger: An Analysis of Concepts of Pollution and Taboo* (New York: Routledge, 2002). My essay in *Aeon* entitled "A Theory of Creepiness" discusses metaphysical threat: https://aeon.co/essays/what-makes-clowns-vampires-and-severed-hands-creepy. There is extensive literature on "monster studies," of variable quality and intelligibility. For a taster, go to Jeffrey Jerome Cohen's edited volume *Monster Theory* (Minneapolis: University of Minnesota Press, 1996). A lucid source for a wide-ranging discussion of monsters is Stephen Asma's *On Monsters: An Unnatural History of Our Worst Fears* (New York: Oxford University Press, 2009). For a fascinating and unusual take on monsters in medieval music, see Anna Zayaruznaya's *The Monstrous New Art: Divided Forms in the Late Medieval Motet* (Cambridge, UK: Cambridge University Press, 2015). Finally, Debra Higgs Strickland's *Saracens, Demons, and Jews: Making Monsters in Medieval Art* (Princeton, NJ: Princeton University Press, 2003) is a good resource of the monsterfication of the other in medieval art.

TWENTY-THREE: CRIMINALS

For the notion that Black people are inherently criminal, see Khalil Gibran Muhammed's *The Condemnation of Blackness: Race, Crime, and the Making of Modern Urban America* (Cambridge, MA: Harvard University Press, 2011). A classic analysis of the construction of the Black male as rapist is Jacquelyn Dowd Hall's "'The Mind That Burns in Each Body': Women, Rape, and Racial Violence," in A. Snitow, C. Stansell, and S. Thompson (Eds.), *Powers of Desire: The Politics of Sexuality* (New York: Monthly Review Press, 1983), 328–349. This can be profitably read in conjunction with Tommy Curry's *The Man Not: Race, Class, Genre, and the Dilemmas of Black Manhood* (Philadelphia: Temple University Press, 2017). There are many historical examples of the racialized and dehumanized being accused of inherent criminality—for example, Jews, as described in Michael Berkowitz's *The Crime of My Very Existence: Nazism and the Myth of Jewish Criminality* (Berkeley: University of California Press, 2007). For the superpredator scare of the 1990s, see John Delulio, "The Coming of the Superpredators," *Weekly Standard* (November 27, 1995), https://www.weeklystandard.com/john-j-dilulio-jr/the-coming-of-the-super-predators. Sarah Burns makes the argument that the image of the Central Park Five was cast in the mold of the Black beast and the attitude of Trump, Buchanan, and others was that of a lynch mob in her book *The Central Park Five: A Chronicle of a City Wilding* (New York: Alfred A. Knopf, 2011).

TWENTY-FOUR: CRUELTY

For the complicated matter of Woodrow Wilson's relationship with *The Birth of a Nation*, see Mark Benbow's "The Birth of a Quotation: Woodrow Wilson and 'Like Writing History with Lightning,'" *Journal of the Gilded Age and Progressive Era* 9, no. 4 (2010): 509–533. For the rebirth of the Ku Klux Klan in 1916, read Linda Gordon's *The Second Coming of the KKK: The Ku Klux Klan of the 1920s and the American Political Tradition* (New York: Liveright, 2017); and Patricia Bernstein's *The First Waco Horror: The Lynching of Jesse Washington and the Rise of the NAACP* (College Station: Texas A & M University Press, 2006). For more context, read William Carrigan's *The Making of a Lynching Culture: Violence and Vigilantism in Central Texas, 1836–1916* (Champaign: University of Illinois Press, 2006). For a contemporary account by the great W. E. B. DuBois, visit this article: "Read W. E. B. DuBois' Brilliant, Horrifying Account of the Real Life Lynching Described in BlacKkKlansman," *Slate*, August 11, 2018, https://slate.com/culture/2018/08/blackkklansman-read-w-e-b-du-bois-account-of-the-real-life-lynching-described-in-the-film.html. For the demonization of Jews and Muslims in medieval Christian Europe, go to Debra Higgs Strickland's *Saracens, Demons, and Jews: Making Monsters in Medieval Art* (Princeton, NJ: Princeton University Press, 2003);

and for the demonizing of Jews from ancient times to the present, see Joel Carmichael's *The Satanizing of the Jews: Origin and Development of Mystical Anti-Semitism* (New York: Fromm International, 1992). For demonization in contemporary international relations, you can read Linn Normand's *Demonization in International Politics: A Barrier to Peace in the Israeli-Palestinian Conflict* (New York: Palgrave, 2016). For a powerful account of cruelty, from a victim of torture, you can do no better than Jean Améry's *At the Mind's Limits: Contemplations by a Survivor on Auschwitz and Its Realities* (Bloomington: Indiana University Press, 2009).

TWENTY-FIVE: DEHUMANIZATION AND ITS NEIGHBORS

For simianization, including the simianization of the Irish and the Japanese, go to W. D. Hund, C. W. Mills, and S. Sebastiani (Eds.), *Simianization: Apes, Gender, Class, and Race* (Zürich: Lit Verlag, 2015). I do not have anything approaching expert knowledge of sexism, ableism, and transphobia, but I can recommend some texts that I and others have found to be especially helpful. There is a very extensive and wide-ranging feminist literature on sexism. A couple of texts especially relevant to the topics of this book are Linda LeMoncheck's *Dehumanizing Women: Treating Persons as Sex Objects* (New York: Rowman and Littlefield, 1985); and Ann Cahill's *Overcoming Objectification* (New York: Routledge, 2011). For the baleful influence of sexism in science, Angela Saini's book *Inferior: How Science Got Women Wrong and the New Research That's Rewriting the Story* (Boston: Beacon Press, 2017) is a terrific read. For a deeper account of disability and ableism, go to Shelley Tremain's edited volume *Foucault and the Government of Disability* (Ann Arbor: University of Michigan Press, 2015); and Elizabeth Barnes's *The Minority Body: A Theory of Disability* (New York: Oxford University Press, 2016). For an engaging and accessible introduction to issues around nonbinary gender identity, read Robin Dembroff's *Aeon* article "Why Be Non-Binary?" October 30, 2018, https://aeon.co/essays/nonbinary-identity-is-a-radical-stance-against-gender-segregation; and for a fascinating take on transphobia, focusing on issues pertinent to this book, read Talia May Bettcher's "Evil

Deceivers and Make-Believers: On Transphobic Violence and the Politics of Illusion," *Hypatia* 22, no. 3 (2007): 43–65.

TWENTY-SIX: RESISTING

There are many publications that deal—explicitly or implicitly—with resisting destructive ideological forces. Much of this material is pertinent to resisting dehumanization. I recommend Timothy Snyder's *On Tyranny: Twenty Lessons from the Twentieth Century* (New York: Tim Duggan Books, 2017); Jason Stanley's *How Fascism Works: The Politics of Us and Them* (New York: Random House, 2017); and Ibram Kendi's *How to Be an Anti-Racist* (New York: One World, 2019).

INDEX

For the benefit of digital users, indexed terms that span two pages (e.g., 52–53) may, on occasion, appear on only one of those pages.